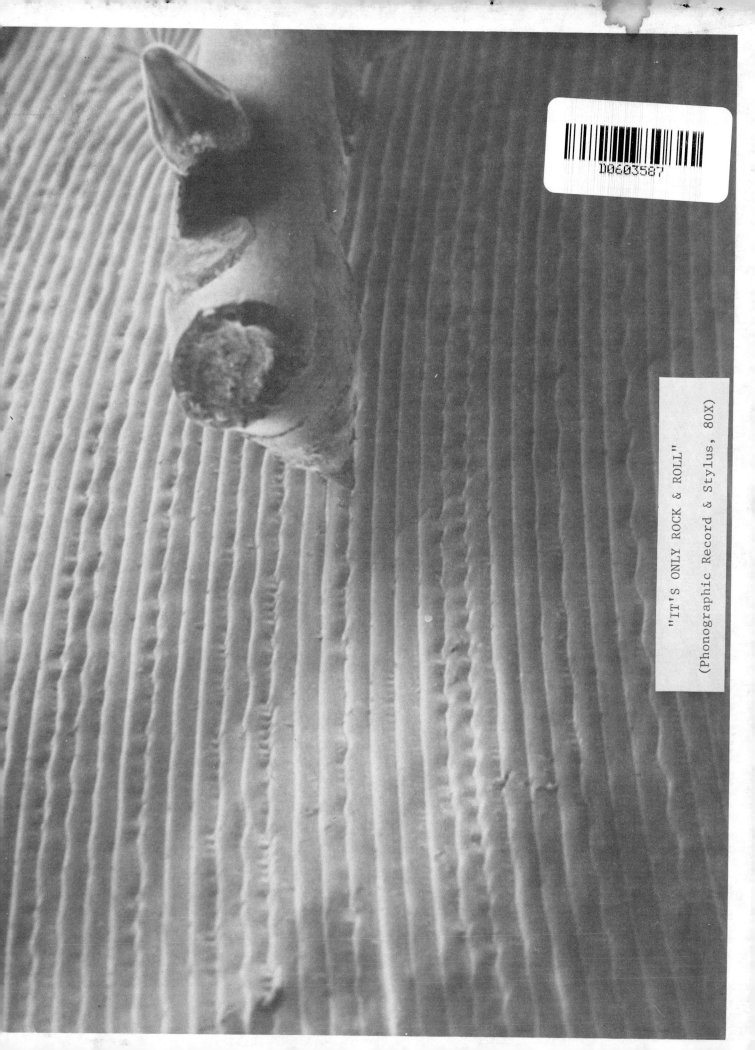

"IT'S ONLY ROCK & ROLL"

(Phonographic Record & Stylus, 80X)

STORY
OF
MUSIC

THE BAGPIPER, *from a woodcut by Albrecht Durer*

THE PANTHEON **STORY OF MUSIC** FOR YOUNG PEOPLE

BY JOSEPH WECHSBERG

PANTHEON BOOKS

designed by Arnold Skolnick

First Printing

Library of Congress Catalog Card Number: 67-20221

Manufactured in the United States of America

THE TROUBADOR, *by the nineteenth-century French painter Honoré Daumier.*

PROLOGUE

Who "invented" music? We shall never know. But we believe that the first music was a song sung by the human voice. People have always used their voices to express their feelings—their joy or sadness. Think of the psalms that King David sang to praise God; of the congregations chanting in church; of the early Negro spirituals expressing the suffering and hope of those people. All this is music.

The first paintings we know of were created by man during the Stone Age, perhaps 60,000 B.C. But the origin of music cannot be stated precisely. Unlike a painting or a sculpture that everyone can see, music must be performed to be heard and experienced. A song, a piano piece "live" only as long as we hear them—then they are gone. People have looked at statues for thousands of years. But only a hundred years ago, there existed no phonograph, no tape recorder, no radio, no juke box. People couldn't hear music just by pushing a button or turning a knob as they can today.

Even today, not many young people have an opportunity to study music at home or in school. Relatively few people have learned to read written music. Only highly trained musicians can "hear" the music just by reading a musical score. A famous conductor once told me that he hears the music in his "inner ear." Another admitted that he reads musical scores in bed before falling asleep the way other people read mystery stories. But the great majority of people appreciate music only when it is performed—and that goes both for classical and popular music.

Music means different things to different people. To some, music is the sound that comes from a radio or record player while doing homework, or reading a book, or playing, or dreaming. To others, music means an evening at the concert hall, the organ in church, the rhythms of jazz, an opera on television, a concerto recorded by Heifetz, Casals, or Rubinstein.

Music, every kind of music, is always alive. It is perhaps closer to our heart than any other art. A song of love needs no words; it can be expressed in sound. In the days of the silent motion pictures, certain basic emotions—love, hatred, jealousy, misery, and fear—were "underscored" by music. When the final chase began on the screen—the hero pursuing the villain who was riding fast, holding the lovely girl tight and threatening to kill her—the piano player in the tiny orchestra pit would quickly switch to Rossini's *William Tell* overture and the audience—no matter in what part of the world the picture was shown—would immediately know what was going to happen.

Music has a truly universal meaning. It affects young and old, men and women; it makes them cheerful or sad; it is something they need. There is hardly a home where the sound of music—at least *some* sound—is not heard during the day; there are places—elevators, hotel lobbies, planes—where we are surrounded by the sound of music, whether we like it or not.

Music is a rewarding art. It will give most to those who try to understand it. It makes no difference whether you prefer Bach or jazz, Mozart or swing, the rhythms of the Beatles or a Beethoven symphony. If you begin to love music, you will discover it as you go along. You will want to know more about music—who wrote it, how it should be played. In the end you will want to play music yourself, and you will be amply rewarded. Can there be anything more beautiful than singing a song? Well, performing music is always a little like singing a song.

The Bible, one of our earliest sources of information about music, tells us that music played an important part in the daily and religious life of the Hebrews. Here the sixteenth-century Flemish master Lucas van Leyden shows David singing one of his psalms for King Saul. He accompanies himself on the harp.

9

PART I
THE ANCIENT WORLD

THE EARLIEST MUSIC

THE earliest sounds of music seem to have come from the Eastern part of the world. The inhabitants of ancient Mesopotamia, the area between the Euphrates and the Tigris rivers known today as Iraq, played various instruments. During the excavations of Ur, the capital of the Sumerians who lived 3000 B.C. in Ur, Nineveh, and Babylon, fragments of harps and lyres were discovered, as well as bas-reliefs with concert scenes.

Music was also a well-known art in the Egypt of the Pharaohs. Paintings and bas-reliefs, found in the royal tombs, show groups of people performing on musical instruments, very much like our modern orchestra. Furthermore, we know the names and biographical data of the celebrated court musicians of the Pharaohs. They played flutes, cymbals, and harps of various designs. The first known harps had only three or four strings. At the Louvre museum in Paris there is an Egyptian wood painting showing the famous singer Amon (who lived probably 1000 B.C.) playing a harp with ten strings.

Unfortunately we don't know what kind of music these people played nor how it sounded. We have no written record of the sort of music played by the Chaldeans and the Egyptians. We know a little more about early music in China where it was expressed by symbols. These symbols were also used in poetry and to indicate certain ethical and political rules.

Music was not always regarded merely as entertainment or even art as it is today. In the early civilizations of the Near and Far East it was said to have magical power. Music was performed in temples to influence and bewitch the minds of men; it was played during warlike ceremonies and religious manifestations. In China, music was considered as a part of poetry. The movements of the sun, the moon, and the stars were thought to create musical sounds.

Another type of music of ancient origin is Hebrew music. Much of it goes back to the songs and psalms which the Hebrews sang thousands of years before the Christian era. These songs and psalms were written down only much later, and it is now impossible to separate the

10

original from the later additions and changes. In this connection, one must realize that music changes with the times; it is not like a painting or a sculpture that remain the same forever. Music is expressed differently by different people at different times. No one knows exactly how a Mozart symphony sounded when Mozart himself heard it. We *believe* we know how it sounded, but we cannot be sure. And we know much less about the early centuries of music.

ABOVE: *Cymbals have been associated with military music since earliest times, as shown by this 7th century B.C. Assyrian bas-relief.*

FAR LEFT: *Pharoah's serpent.*

LEFT: *A detail from a limestone relief, dating from about 1580 B.C. shows two musicians taking part in a religious ceremony. The musician on the left plays the eight-stringed harp, on the top of which is carved the head of a falcon—the god of harp playing. The flautist holds his instrument in a lateral position.*

OPPOSITE: *A double-aulos player, from a fresco dating from 400 B.C. The aulos, with its shrill and piercing sound was the chief wind instrument used by the Greeks. It is similar to the present-day oboe.*

MUSIC IN ANCIENT GREECE

THE Greeks were mad about music. In fact, music was much more important to them than painting, sculpture, and architecture. We don't know exactly how Greek music sounded but we know what it meant to the people of Greece. Paradoxically, while we know a great deal about the writers of ancient Greece, Homer and Aeschylos, Sophocles and Euripides, we know very little about the composers because no written records exist. Consequently, we now consider ancient Greece a nation of philosophers (Socrates and Plato) or of historians (Thucydides and Herodotus) or of sculptors (Phidias and Praxiteles) but we don't think of it as a nation of musicians.

Yet the Greeks devoted much attention to music. The word "music" is derived from the Greek *Mousa* meaning Muse. Originally there were only three Muses. Two symbolized Study and Memory which are necessary in every art. The third Muse was called Song. Greek songs were sung at rural festivals. They contained a certain rhythm, to be sung perhaps during the threshing. These were popular folk songs. We know that they had a certain rhythm though we don't know what sort of melody there was. Rhythm, which most young people feel instinctively, is the life force of music, the flow of its motion. Rhythm exists everywhere. The recurrent change of day and night, of low and high tide, of summer and winter proves that nature follows the laws of rhythm. Rhythm is essential in music because music is an art that happens in time, not in space like painting and sculpture. The human ear counts rhythm in twos (*one*-two, *one*-two) or in threes (*one*-two-three).

The Greeks had their national instrument, the lyre, which plays an important part in Greek mythology. Perhaps you have read the story of the infant Hermes who killed a turtle and fastened on its shell gut strings made from the entrails of an oxen that he had stolen from his brother Apollo. That, according to myth, was the first lyre. Apollo became angry, and Hermes, trying to appease the older brother, let him use the instrument. Ever since, Apollo has been

12

OPPOSITE: *Greek pottery is an especially rich source of information about music. This vase, dating from the early fifth century B.C. and believed to come from Sicily, depicts a procession of lyre and castanet players.*
BELOW: *A bas-relief showing a young girl playing the double aulos.*

The dance, associated with the cult of Dionysius, was an important part of Greek culture. An aulos player provides the rhythms for this dancing girl.

known as the first virtuoso on the lyre, and the sponsor of ancient Greek music. The center of the Apollo cult was first the island of Delos and later Delphi, in the shadow of Mount Parnassus.

Greek myths tell wonderful stories about great heroes endowed with marvelous musical gifts. There is Orpheus who conquers death by the power of his lyre; after losing his wife he so moved the gods with his music that they permitted him to descend to Hades and bring back his beloved Euridice. The story of Orpheus has been the subject of more operas than any other.

Scholars claim that Asia Minor is the home of yet another national instrument, a primitive reed pipe called aulos, that looked like a small oboe. There exists a fierce mythical conflict between lyre and aulos. The lyre was an attribute of Apollo, the God of sobriety and moderation; whereas the aulos—the instrument of the Phrygian satyr Marsyas—stood for ecstacy. There was a contest between the two, Marsyas was defeated, and as a punishment was flayed. Ancient Greece is a fine hunting ground for detectives of legends and myths.

If you are familiar with the exciting world of ancient mythology, you will have learned that one of the earliest musicians was a blind singer—Thamyris. Homer tells us his boasts so offended the Muses that they blinded him.

Virgil speaks of Misenus who accompanied Aeneas to Italy. He played the trumpet so well that he challenged Triton, a god of the sea, to a competition. Misenus lost and was drowned. The mythological players acted as some of our great virtuosi today who are often in the mood to challenge the gods. The commendable exception among Homer's performers was Phemius who did not challenge anyone. He left the court of Odysseus, went to Smyrna and began to teach music to young people. He was the first music teacher, according to Greek mythology.

The Greeks believed that there was a close relation between sounds of music and the seasons of the year and parts of the day. The cycles of the sun and the moon, birth and death, healing and reincarnation—all were expressed in terms of music. The Greeks thought that music played an important role in the political system and in the education of the young people, because good music was believed to help build character.

In his main work *The Republic*, Plato (427–347 B.C.) considers "music and gymnastics" as the basic elements in education. He claims that music comes first because it helps to perfect the soul, and it is the soul that should help build the body. He says that gymnastics must be tempered

The reclining figure appears overcome by the combined effects of wine and music. He holds his head in a gesture of ecstasy.

14

The Greeks also sang without instrumental accompaniment. Here the performer reads from a scroll held by a servant— a "living" music stand.

by music, otherwise it leads to rowdiness, and that music without gymnastics leads to sagging energy. He recommends that the entire population be divided into large choruses. The first would contain boys, the second young men up to the age of thirty, the third all men from thirty to sixty years of age. In Plato's philosophical system music occupied the leading position among the arts. Plato thought that the aim of music was not merely "entertainment" but "perfection of the soul." It was not a private matter, but a public affair.

In Greece, then, music was considered a serious art and had a solid theoretical foundation. The theory of music—as we know it today—was formulated there in the fourth century B.C. and Aristoxenus of Tarentum (b. 350 B.C.) was the major theoretician of that time whose influence lasted for many centuries.

A few fragments of Greek musical works have been discovered by modern Hellenic scholars. But they are rather short, and it is impossible to say how they were sung and performed and how they sounded. All we know is that the old Greek music was not harmonic or contrapuntal—meaning that it was not written for several voices or parts. The Greeks did not know the principle of polyphony, or "many-voiced music," in which

each voice sings an independent melody. Greek music was monophonic, or "one-voiced" music, and consisted of what we would now consider simple melodies. The listeners followed this "simple" music with great attention; they enjoyed slight "inflections" (changes) of the melodic line. It was very different from today's symphonic music but it achieved the same goal: it was exciting music that inspired and moved the listeners. And that is the ultimate aim of all music, of all art.

Music played an important part in the battles of the ancient Greeks. Herodotus, Plutarch, Thucydides and Gellius often report about military music. We know that Alyattes, the Lydian king, invaded the territory of the Milesians to the sound of the aulos. Plutarch reports that the Lacedaemonians blew the "Castor song" on the auloi before they attacked. Xenophon describes the use of the aulos as a military bugle. The soldiers marched into battle to the sound of the aulos "to retain an orderly grouping of ranks." The Greeks had a deeper reason (and a word) for anything they did. The aulos players were placed at various spots and their prelude was intended to put the soldiers into a fighting mood. Then the "Castor song" gave the sign for the attack.

During the fifth and fourth centuries B.C. the famous aulos players became as popular as the great piano virtuosi of our time. The melodies were no longer simple but overloaded with embellishments. The celebrated Timotheus of Miletus (circa 446–357 B.C.) was much in demand for his dithyrambs (poems) and elaborate lyre playing. The public applauded but the critics took a dim view of such "decadence," as the celebrated scholar Aristoxenus would later describe it. The literary world was divided between friends and foes of the "new" music. Aristophanes, the great satirist, wrote against the new tendency of music because it ruined "the grave, majestic" line of the "old" music— which proves that nothing is new in this world. At the end of the Hellenistic period, there was much confusion in Greek music—not unlike the situation in music today.

THE DECLINE OF MUSIC IN ROME

Most Roman music was simply Greek music performed in Rome. Compared to the exquisite taste of the Greeks, the taste of the Romans was rather vulgar. Ptolemy Philadelphus (d. 246 B.C.) writes about a procession at the court of Alexandria. Six hundred men participated, and three hundred of them played on golden lyres. It must have been a spectacular sight—but perhaps not exactly a feast for the ears. By the time of Augustus (63 B.C.–A.D. 14) the Greek aulos had developed into a very large instrument. Ammianus Marcellinus, a writer and observer of social trends, mentions "lyres as big as chariots," which certainly sounds terrible. Not satisfied with their big instruments, the Romans created large ensembles of them, making terrific noise.

The Romans added various Oriental elements to Greek music. Everything was bigger, though not better, than in ancient Greece. There were large "symphonic" ensembles. Seneca reports that sometimes there were more singers on the stage than listeners in the audience. The singing was supported by many brass instruments, some distributed in strategic spots among the audience; auloi and organs were placed all over the large stage. Entertainment was on a colossal scale. Often there were eight or ten thousand listeners!

The Romans wanted to have fun; they were not concerned with the lofty principles of art. They trained slaves to become performers and professional entertainers. One Chrysogonus was said to have so many musicians among his slaves that the vicinity of his residence reverberated day and night with the racket of instruments and voices. Maecenas, the wealthy Roman statesman and patron of the arts, suffered from insomnia and liked to listen to "soft, distant music." The Emperor Caligula ordered that choruses sing while his galley sailed through the Gulf of Naples. At the famous Roman repasts large choruses performed, accompanied by the castanets of Andalusian dancers.

No one had to pay admission to the big spectacles and new "hit" tunes became known faster than in the twentieth century when radio became popular. Cicero reports of connoisseurs who were able to identify a composition "after the first flute tone." When a singer made a mistake, the public showed its disapproval in a noisy way. The audiences were often so uneducated that concerts of imported Greek musicians had to be made more attractive by such additions as the performance of Roman wrestlers. The Emperor Nero, better remembered to this day for the burning of Rome than for his artistic activities, in 60 A.D. founded "holy" festivals, with music being the most important part of the program. At the end of the first century Emperor Domitian founded "Capitoline games," with poets, musicians, and singers competing. The games—like today's Olympic games—were held every fourth year. The winners received the laurels and prizes from the emperor's own hands. The competing artists came from as far as Africa and Asia. They must have been gifted; most of them composed their own contributions.

The Roman virtuosi studied with renowned singing teachers whose names were often mentioned on their programs. Like today's singers, they were afraid of bad weather, and sang their scales daily. Loud singing became very popular. Some singers shouted so lustily that they suffered ruptured blood vessels from the exertion. But those who survived the ordeal earned much fame, money, and even power. Horace mentions that the famous singer Tigellius had the nerve to turn down the request of Emperor Augustus. The famous virtuosi had their own cheer leaders, and there were jealousies and intrigues much worse than among today's prima donnas.

Originally, the Romans just wanted to have fun and were not interested in musical theory. But by the time of Marcus Terentius Varro (116–27? B.C.) the science of music was an "element of education." Nero and Britannicus had very good musical training, according to Seneca and Suetonius. Marcus Aurelius mentions that teachers of his time were proficient in geometry and music. Several Roman emperors —Hadrian, Caracalla, Antoninus Pius, Heliogabalus and Alexander Severus—were skilled singers and played the cithara, the tuba and the

water organ. According to the legend, Nero in his dying hour exclaimed, *"Qualis artifex pereo!"*—"What an artist is lost in me!"

ABOVE: *A Roman military bugle.* OPPOSITE: *Music manuscripts were scarce in ancient times, but the enthusiasm of the performers was great, as this relief by the fifteenth-century artist Luca della Robbia vividly portrays.* BELOW: *This wall painting from 100 B.C. shows a lady of the nobility playing the cithara—an ancient Greek stringed instrument resembling the lyre.*

BYZANTINE MUSIC

WE know much less about music during the early Christian era than we know about Greek music at the time of Aristoxenus. Music no longer inspired writers and philosophers. The focal point of Eastern Christendom was Byzantium—later named Constantinople and the seat of the Holy Roman Empire.

While the Greeks had developed the aulos and the lyre, the Byzantines had only the organ, which was important in their "court music." The organ appears in bas-reliefs of the first centuries after the beginning of the Christian Era. Byzantine music, like all Oriental music, was performed "in unison," everybody singing the same tune which was also played by the organ. The reports of travelers speak of gold organs but we know little about the nature of the organ accompaniment. The Byzantines liked to have music at their festivals, family reunions, and nuptials. They loved to show off with organ music when "barbarians," i.e., foreigners, were around.

Byzantine instrument makers were very famous. The musical automatons at the imperial throne room were much admired by foreign ambassadors and barbarian guests. The emperors were particularly proud of statues of lions near their thrones which contained ingenious instruments that would imitate the lion's roar. That should give you the idea of Byzantine entertainment. The organ was considered an instrument of "secular" music, which is not church music, but "worldly." Only after it was introduced into the Western world, did the organ become an instrument of the Church. Much of the music performed in the imperial palace was, not unexpectedly, "praise songs" for the emperor. As long as the artist extolled the ruler's virtues, he couldn't go wrong.

There was also much church music. The Eastern Church (in Greece and Turkey) still retains many "liturgical" (or sacred) works composed fifteen hundred years ago. The music is simple, almost monotonous; after the third century there were some hymns. Greek was then the official church language, and the first part of the Catholic Mass still begins with a Greek invocation, *Kyrie eleison!* (O Lord, have mercy!)

18

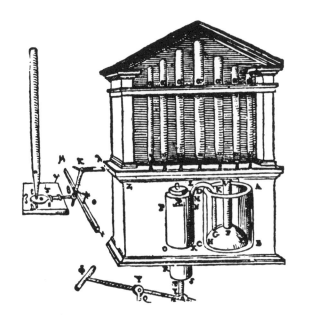

LEFT: *Heron's water organ. The mechanics of organ building appears to have fascinated Byzantine instrument makers. Describing the instrument, one contemporary observer wrote: "I see a strange species of reeds . . . a blast, rushing forth from a cavern of bull's hide, forces its way from beneath . . . and a skillful man having nimble fingers stands feeling the yielding rods of pipes, and they, gently dancing, press out song."*

OPPOSITE: *Muscle as well as musicianship was required to play the medieval organ. The organist had to pull out a slide at the base of a pipe, thereby allowing air to rush in and sound a tone.*

BELOW: *Teamwork was also needed to perform on the medieval organ, as this illustration from a twelfth-century manuscript humorously shows.*

PART II
MIDDLE AGES & RENAISSANCE

GREGORIAN CHANT & EARLY NOTATION

ABOVE: *A woodcut from the late fifteenth century shows Saint Gregory instructing two pupils in the chant. The dove on his shoulder represents the Holy Ghost, by whose inspiration (according to legend) he is said to have collected the melodies that bear his name.* OPPOSITE: *This handsome carved-ivory manuscript cover from the ninth or tenth century, shows the* schola cantorum *taking part in the service of the Mass.*

DURING the early Christian Era almost all music we know of was church or "liturgical" music. Of course there was as much secular, popular, and folk music as at any other time, but it was never written down, and the learned monks never did mention it. Therefore we know nothing about it. But about sacred music we know a good deal. Usually the early psalms were sung by a soloist. Sometimes the congregation would end with an *Alleluia!* or a refrain sung in unison. This is not a Christian invention. Recent discoveries prove that this opposition between soloist and chorus was already known in ancient Egypt. In the fourth century the congregation began to sing the whole psalm in two choirs which sang alternately, one after the other. This was known as antiphony (the origin of the word "anthem," which used to indicate the refrain sung by *both* choirs). It is thought—but it has not been proven —that one choir consisted of men, and the other of women and children singing one octave higher. In Greek musical theory antiphony means a one-octave interval.

From the fifth to the ninth century, during the Barbarian invasions, church music remained unaffected, while kingdoms broke down. But the churches of Milan, Rome, France, and Spain had developed their own kinds of chant. The great reformer of church music was Pope Gregory I (540–604) who has been called "the Great." For centuries Gregory was credited with having made a standard collection of sacred songs which are still called Gregorian Chant. Perhaps he only codified reforms that had started earlier and were to be continued by later popes. It is also believed that Gregory reorganized the famous *schola cantorum* (school of singers) in Rome. He wanted to be sure that there would always be enough trained singers in the papal choir. Some of them he probably sent to other churches as teachers. Such schools were established in all church centers in Europe.

It would be wrong to think of the *schola cantorum* as a school in our sense of the word. People hadn't learned to write music yet; musical notation did not exist. In the seventh century, Isidore of Seville wrote, "Unless retained by the memory sounds perish, for they cannot be written down."

Something had to be done to train the memory of the young singers. At the beginning of the ninth century musical manuscripts contain *neumes*—from the Greek word *neuma* which means "figure" or "sign." The *neumes* are little signs, lines, or points that were placed above the text, as a kind of musical shorthand, to remind the singer of the music that he had memorized. After the ninth century these *neumes* were used in several countries. The earliest notes consist of the *virga*, a line rising obliquely from left to right parallel with the script; and the *punctum*, a descending line that was later reduced to a point. The *virga* signified that the voice must rise, the *punctum* that it must descend; but the signs didn't say how far the voice should rise or descend.

In the tenth century further progress was made. Italian copyists had the idea of drawing a line, called staff, that signified a certain pivotal (main) note in the middle register of the melody. Suppose the line would mean the note "A." Then the higher sounds would be written above it, and the lower sounds underneath. For the first time, the vocal line could be "seen." This was the beginning of the principle of "diastemic" notation (from the Greek word *diastema*, or interval) which still exists in our modern system of writing musical notation.

The system was not accurate though. The singers had learned their repertory by heart but, after all, it was not a complicated repertory. Gradually, the system was improved. A second line was added at the interval of a fifth, then a third and a fourth line, all drawn in different colors. (For instance, the "F" was red, the "C" was yellow.) By the end of the twelfth century a four-line staff was generally used. Each line was marked at the beginning by a letter corresponding to the note it represented. From these letters the "clefs" were derived; colored lines were no longer used. These fascinating inventions were said to have been created mainly by Guido d'Arezzo (980?–1050), the great musical theoretician of the Middle Ages.

An example of Gregorian notation from an early eleventh-century manuscript. The rubric at the top tells us that this is an Introit to be performed at Mass on the fourth Sunday before Christmas.

Until the eighth century the first six notes of the scale had been designated by letters. Guido d'Arezzo had the idea of adding to each letter the first syllable of a verse from the hymn to St. John the Baptist: *Ut* queant laxis/ *Re*sonare fibris/*Mi*ra gestorum/*Fa*muli tuorum,/*Sol*ve polluti/*La*bii reatum,/Sancte Iohannes! Each verse of this hymn began on a note that was one tone higher than the preceding verse; the fourth was separated from the third by a semitone. Now the singer could learn the intervals by name—the tones and the semitone ut, re, mi, fa, sol, la. This "hexachord" (a Greek word meaning "series of six notes") became the basis of "solmization" (from the notes sol and mi), meaning a system of designating the degrees of the scale by the use of syllables. This later led to our present system. The history of musical notation is truly fascinating and rewarding.

Pope Gregory had laid down the law for the proper performance of sacred music. This was important but dangerous. If his codification were to stand unchanged forever, there was the possibility that the music could never develop. Guido d'Arezzo was the first scholar who established the superiority of the *musicus* (or composer) over the *cantor* (or singer). He used to say, "He who does not know what he is doing, is by definition a beast." He meant that the composer *created* music; the singer only performed what the composer created. Today this important difference is often forgotten. On our record albums the names of prominent singers and conductors are often printed in larger letters than the composer's name. Yet without the composer there would be no music—and no records.

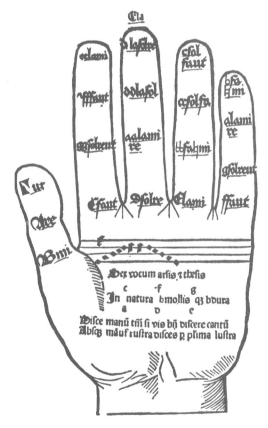

Guido of Arezzo (980–1050) devised this ingenious method—the Guidonian hand—to aid sight singing. He divided the scale into six tones—the hexachord—ut, re, mi, fa, sol, la. Using his hand, the choir leader could show the choir-boys the correct pitch. Guido claimed that with his method, a singer could learn in five months what had previously taken ten years.

This beautifully illuminated manuscript shows Gregorian notation at a high stage of development. While the rhythm of the piece is still uncertain, lines and clefs (the diamond-shaped symbols at the left) make the pitches of the melody clear. The diamond-shaped note at the end of each line is called a custos. It is not sung, but is placed there to tell the singer the pitch on which the next line is to start.

THE TROUBADOURS

Music owes a lot to Charlemagne who was crowned Holy Roman Emperor in the year 800. He brought trained singers from Rome and established many music schools in his empire. In the century following his death two innovations were created, the "sequence" and the "trope."

In both cases new words were added to the fixed text of the Gregorian Chant in order to support a florid melody sung on the same syllable. Thus, the Alleluia traditionally ended on a long melodic flourish sung on the last syllable *-a*. Now a "sequence" of words was invented to be sung with this melody. The usage lasted for half a century and we owe to it some of the great hymns, such as the *Stabat mater* and the *Dies irae*. The tropes were similar additions, this time within the text of the chant to support an ornamental melody, for instance between the two words *Kyrie* and *eleison*.

Both these developments reflect perhaps a popular influence. (The native monks felt uncomfortable singing florid "oriental" melodies.) Of the secular music of the early Middle Ages, however, we know practically nothing.

Dance music was performed by *jongleurs* ("jugglers") who were buffoons and renegades (runaways) from the Church, and worldly, sometimes bawdy songs were sung by the *goliards*, itinerant clerics or students who preferred their free life to strict discipline inside a monastery. The goliards roamed all over Europe, performing their catchy tunes with texts in debased Latin and accompanying themselves with a few notes on a harp or hurdy-gurdy (*vielle*). Jugglers and goliards came from all classes of society; some were French or Breton, others were English or Scandinavian.

By the end of the eleventh century the *troubadours* began to appear. They were either noblemen who stayed at home or itinerant singers who wandered from castle to castle. The troubadours were native to Provence, the sun-drenched, colorful south of France. (Some scholars claim that Aquitania, which included the province of Limoges was really the cradle of the troubadours.) The *trouvères* were the

ABOVE: *Four troubadours playing castenets, harp, rebec, and drum. From a fifteenth-century French illustration.*
BELOW: *Israel von Meckenen (d. 1503) treats the Biblical story of Salome and John the Baptist in this canvas titled* THE DANCE OF HEROD. *The musicians (left to right) play the Zink, flute and drum, and the trombone.*
OPPOSITE: *An illustration from Decameron—*THE PROCESSION TO THE GARDEN. *A lute player leads the way. Fourteenth century.*

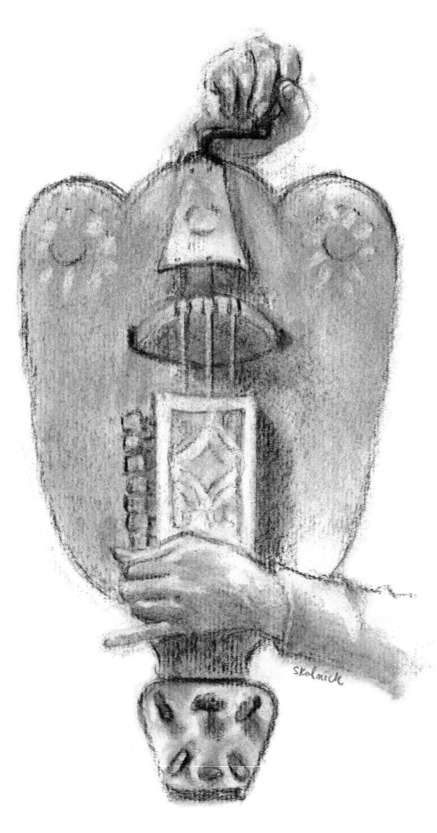

A hurdy-gurdy, or German lyre.

northern counterparts of the troubadours.

The troubadours flourished between 1150 and 1210 when French literature dominated western Europe. Even Italian poets wrote in Provençal, the language of Provence. Dante himself once thought of writing his great epic poem *The Divine Comedy* in the language of the troubadours. At this time the great feudal lords formed a new society in Europe. Their culture was separate from that of the Church. They loved wars and tournaments, admired honor and revered women. The troubadours wrote their own songs about these heroic knights. Troubadours were not ordinary "performers"; most of them were men of noble birth who believed in "art for the sake of art." They composed beautiful verse and music. Their inspiration came both from the music of the Christian world, and from the tunes of the jongleurs and goliards. The famous troubadours had wonderful names: Blondel de Nesle, King of Navarre, Gillebert de Berneville.

After the Norman Conquest in 1066, many troubadours (and minstrels) came to England, and appeared at the castles of the nobility or at court festivals. At the end of the thirteenth century they even formed a corporation in Yorkshire that became quite wealthy during the reign of Henry VI (1422–1461).

Many songs of the troubadours are preserved. The notation of the music records the melody but not the rhythm. We know how they sounded but not in what tempo they were sung. The singers knew their repertory by heart and needed only the melody on paper; *they* knew how to sing it. In Germany, a similar movement began at the time of Emperor Frederick Barbarossa in the twelfth century. There the artists were called minnesinger or minnesänger (*"minne"* means love and *"singen"* to sing) and they sang of courtly love. First they adapted the works of the French troubadours but soon they developed their own art. The most famous of them were Wolfram von Eschenbach and Walther von der Vogelweide; both lived between 1170 and 1220. If you attend a performance of Wagner's popular opera *Tannhäuser* (which has the

26

subtitle "The Singers' War at the Wartburg") you will see the famous minnesänger taking part in a mythical war at a castle in Thuringia.

The tradition of the minnesänger was continued in the fifteenth and sixteenth centuries by the Meistersinger (mastersingers), members of the burgher class (not the aristocracy) who had their composing and singing schools. In his beautiful, comic opera *The Mastersingers of Nuremberg*, Richard Wagner has given a lively portrait of the members of such a school. An apprentice would start out as a "pupil" before he could become a "school's friend," a "poet," or a "master," the highest rank given to one who could both create a poem and the music that went with it. They gave the tones strange names, such as "blue tone," "rose tone," "black-as-ink tone," "warbler's tone." The melodies were slow and embellished. The hero of Wagner's opera (and an authentic great Meistersinger) was Hans Sachs, "cobbler and poet." (In the opera Sachs helps lovely Eva, the daughter of his friend Pogner, the town's goldsmith, to win the heart of a young nobleman named Walther von Stolzing. Stolzing is a follower of Walther von der Vogelweide and refuses to accept the dictates of the Mastersingers —but all ends well.)

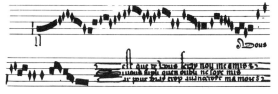

ABOVE: *A Poetical and Musical Congress at Wartburg in 1207. The minnesingers assembled are Walther von der Vogelweide, Wolfram von Eschenbach, Reinmar of Zweter, Henry called the Virtuous Writer, Henry of Ofterdingen, and Klingsor of Hungary. From a fourteenth-century manuscript.* LEFT: *A fragment from a troubadour song.*

27

THE RISE OF POLYPHONY (ARS ANTIQUA)

ALL the music we have mentioned so far whether sacred or secular was "monophonic." There was only one melody and even if the troubadours or minnesänger accompanied their singing the accompaniment was the same melody played on an instrument.

Sometime before the year 1000—we do not know exactly when or where—people began to sing in two parts. At first, however, the two voices sang in strictly parallel motion at the distance of a fifth. The next step was to begin in unison, then diverge up to the interval of a fourth, continue at this interval, and converge again for the conclusion. This two-part singing was called organum; we do not know why, but the term had nothing to do with the organ. Such polyphony may sound crude and primitive to us, and yet it is the beginning of music as we know it today.

Slowly the rigid scheme was abandoned and the two parts began to move more independently. A first high point was reached by Leonin in Paris in the twelfth century. In his *Great Book of Organum* he still used only two parts, but in the next generation Perotin added one or two additional parts to these organa and composed others in three or four parts. In all these compositions the melodic backbone was always a Gregorian Chant. To lengthen the composition the chant was stretched out; each of its notes was held for a very long time. This was impractical for the human voice, therefore it is assumed the part was usually played on an instrument.

These beginnings of polyphony are called Ars Antiqua (Old Art); its last important master was Adam de la Halle (1240–1287), who also was the last troubadour. In his biblical and secular "musical plays" he did not, however, use polyphony. His delightful *Play of Robin and Marion* is again being performed today. The most famous medieval sacred play is the *Play of Daniel*, which originated in the cathedral of Beauvais in about 1150, and is still occasionally performed.

A word must now be said about the sounds

that are being used in music, whether composed or traditional. Gregorian Chant was (and still is) sung in the so-called church modes. These modes ultimately came from ancient Greek music and are still called by Greek names. Very roughly, they correspond to the scales starting on C, D, E, etc. when played on the white keys of the piano. If you listen closely you will hear that each of the scales has a different character which is due to the placement of the semitone intervals (E/F and B/C). Two of the scales, those starting on C and on A, correspond to our major and minor keys, giving rise to the concept of tonality. For centuries all music was composed in the modal system, with the tonal system slowly making headway until it began to reign supreme at the beginning of the Baroque Age. Modality, however, was never completely forgotten. You may have wondered about certain titles, such as the Doric Fugue by Bach (written in the Dorian mode) or the "Lydian mode" mentioned in Beethoven's string quartet, opus 132. When we reach the present in this book you will see that at the beginning of our century, tonality in turn began to give way to new concepts of sound organization which, for want of a better term, is widely called atonality. Most of us have been raised within the system of tonality which is the language common to Bach and Gershwin. Anything not composed in this familiar language may sound strange or exotic or primitive or obstruse or boring to us. In such cases the fault lies with us, not the music.

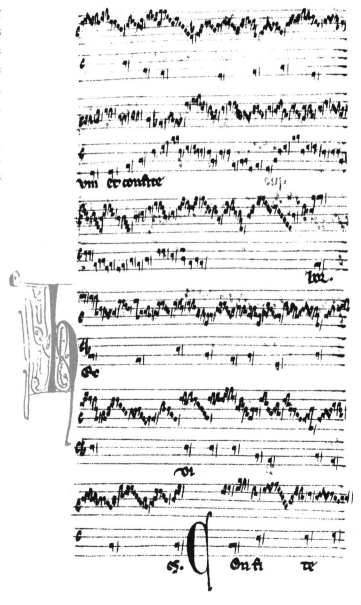

OPPOSITE: *Music manuscripts were scarce and expensive. Those that existed had to be designed so that many singers could use the same book. This woodcut from a musical treatise of the early sixteenth century (Gafurius,* Pratica musicae, *Venice, 1512) shows the crowded conditions that must have prevailed.*

RIGHT: *An early and famous example of two-part sacred music, the Easter gradual* Haec dies, *attributed to the twelfth-century composer Leonin. The Gregorian melody (the cantus firmus) is played or sung (or both) in long, sustained tones, while above it a highly ornamented and rhythmically complex melody is performed. This two-part organum is preserved in a manuscript from Wolfenbuttel, Germany.*

ARS NOVA

Luca della Robbia's CHOIR.

PHILIPPE de Vitry (1291–1361) was the author of a treatise called *Ars Nova* (*New Art*) which was concerned with the notation of rhythm. Obviously, polyphonic music demanded a precise notation of rhythmical values, and during its rise a system of "mensural" notation was slowly developed and first established around 1250 by Franco of Cologne. De Vitry further improved and refined the system. The celebrated Italian poet Petrarch wrote a long letter in 1350 paying homage to de Vitry, "the French musician . . . the greatest, the only poet of his period." Too few of de Vitry's compositions have survived to form an opinion of him as a composer. Therefore the Ars Nova is preserved for us mainly in the works of Guillaume de Machaut (1300–1377), the greatest composer of his century. Born in Champagne, he became a cleric and was employed as secretary to the king of Bohemia. In the train of his master he traveled in many parts of eastern Europe. Later he settled in Reims, and most of his compositions seem to date from this period. The bulk of his work consists of lively and refined secular songs, often with instrumental accompaniment. He was the first to use syncopation (shift of the accent to the unaccented part of the measure) and triplets (three notes in the time of two). In his work we detect the beginning of modern tonality as such— melodies that are clearly conceived in the key of C major. Perhaps his greatest achievement was his *Messe de Notre Dame*. It was the first complete setting of the mass by one man. Here Machaut used a device which proved fertile in the organization of large works: the whole mass is developed out of one motif.

No wonder the Ars Nova, coming from France, soon created discussions and reverberations in neighboring Italy. This was a time when the arts were greatly admired, the time of Giotto, of Dante, of Petrarch, and Simone Martini. Now Florentine composers joined the painters and the poets. The most famous musician of the period was Francesco Landini (1325–1397) who was the son of a painter. Afflicted with blindness from childhood he became an admired organist, composer, poet, and philosopher. His fame as organist of San Lorenzo in Florence was legendary. He could tune an organ and take it apart "down to the last pipe." But he was also a famous flutist and lute player.

His contemporary Giovanni di Prato tells how one day "a thousand birds" were singing in the garden, and Landini was asked to accompany them on the *organetto* (a small hand organ) to see whether the birds would become silent. "At first," writes Giovanni, "the birds were almost silent in order to listen to him. Afterwards they sang with greater brilliance than ever, while a nightingale settled on the branch of a tree just above his head."

Landini's compositions were written in the form of madrigal, ballad, and chasse. The madrigal was a secular song of two or three strophes with a *ritornello* (conclusion) at the end, written for two or three voices. The *ballata* (the Italian word for ballad) consists of many verses that are sung to the same tune. The *chasse* or *caccia* (French and Italian for "hunt") are long songs that describe either exciting street scenes, or hunting and fishing adventures, with the single voices "chasing" each other with great animation. Apparently the composers had already attained virtuoso effects.

BELOW: *This tapestry, called* THE TRIUMPH OF ETERNITY, *comes from France and was woven during the first decade of the sixteenth century. Angels play the most popular instruments of the period—harp, lute, organ, and flute.*

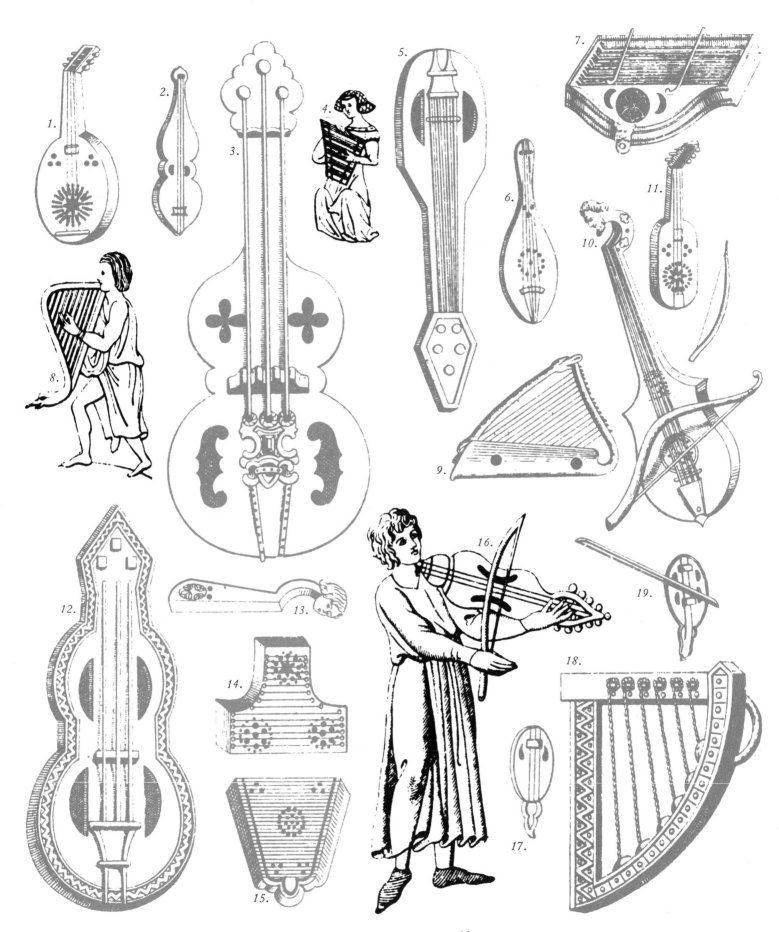

From paintings made at that time we know that many instruments were already in use: viols, harps, psalteries, lutes, hurdy-gurdies, trumpets, drums, chimes, cymbals, bagpipes, reeds, horns, and flutes. The favorite instrument was the viol, but the organ was also quite popular, in the form of either a stationary "chamber organ" or the portative organ that could be carried around. The organist was the most experienced musician, holding together the ensemble of the players, and playing interludes between the singing, thus enabling the singers to catch their breath. The ensembles often consisted of a dozen or more members, each playing a different instrument.

While the Italian Ars Nova was inspired by French models, an independent development seems to have taken place in England. On the continent, polyphony had started by using the intervals of the fourth and the fifth, and the Church favored this style for a long time because they were acoustically the most perfect intervals. But in England popular polyphony preferred the intervals of third and sixth which even to our ears have a sweeter sound than the stark fourths and fifths. And there is an early example of a very melodious and harmonious piece of this music coming from England, the famous round *Sumer is icumen in*. It was out of this local tradition that the first great English composer, John Dunstable (1370–1453), arose. In the service of Prince John, Duke of Bedford, Regent of France, he lived many years in Paris and thus had considerable influence on the development of French music, especially through his friend Guillaume Dufay.

Musical Instruments of the 12th–16th Centuries

1. Cittern (16th c.)	13. Cittern (14th c.)
2. Cittern (12th c.)	14. Harp (14th c.)
3. Viol (12th c.)	15. Harp (12th c.)
4. Psalterion (16th c.)	16. Viol (14th c.)
5. Viol (12th c.)	17. Viol (13th c.)
6. Cittern (14th c.)	18. Harp (12th c.)
7. Harp (16th c.)	19. Viol. (13th c.)
8. Harp (12th c.)	20. Double flute (16th c.)
9. Harp (12th c.)	21. Viol (12th c.)
10. Viol (16th c.)	22. Portative organ (16th c.)
11. Viol (14th c.)	23. Chalumeau (14th c.)
12. Viol (12th c.)	

THE FRANCO-FLEMISH MASTERS

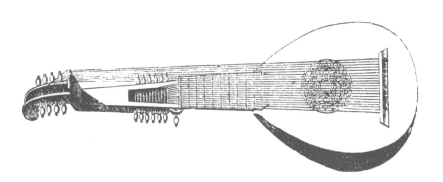

ABOVE: *The lute was the most widely used instrument throughout the Renaissance. It came in many sizes and with a varying number of strings, but its basic design remained unchanged. It could serve as a solo, accompanying, or ensemble instrument.*
OPPOSITE: ANGELS SINGING AND PLAYING, *by the Brothers Van Eyck (1432). Here we see the singing angels on the left gathered around one music book. The angels on the right provide the accompaniment, playing the organ, harp, and viol.*

HISTORIANS like to say that the fall of Constantinople in 1453 marks the end of the Middle Ages, and the beginning of the Renaissance—which is a sort of buffer period between the Middle Ages and our modern times. The discovery of America in 1492 is considered another important date. Today the term "Renaissance" is synonymous with Italy. But Italy did not produce a single great composer during this time; it imported its musicians from northern Europe. For several generations most great composers came from what was then Burgundy, a region extending from the north of France to the south of Holland. These composers consolidated the French-English tradition and in their travels spread this style all over Europe. The first great master was Dunstable's friend, Guillaume Dufay (1400–1474). He was trained at the center of Burgundian church music, the cathedral of Cambrai, but then spent many years in Italy where he absorbed the Italian Ars Nova.

Dufay wrote many secular songs of great refinement as well as many beautiful masses. Here he made a revolutionary innovation: he abandoned the Gregorian Chant as the melodic backbone and used instead popular songs; and in one of his last works, an *Ave Regina*, he introduced a personal note by adding to the liturgical text his own trope, "Have mercy on your dying Dufay." Dufay's close contemporary, Gilles Binchois (1400–1460), was also trained at Cambrai, and is remembered for his charming and sometimes very sad secular songs for solo voice and instrumental accompaniment.

Dufay's most famous disciple was Johannes Ockeghem (1430–1495) from Flanders. From the age of twenty-three to his death he was in the service of the kings of France in Paris and Tours. He composed chiefly church music, especially masses. He had an astonishing gift for counterpoint and was the first to make systematic use of imitative counterpoint, in which certain motivic inflections in the main part of the composition recur in the other parts, thus giving the work great cohesion. The other master of this second generation is Jacob Obrecht

DEO LAVS DÑENIS ORAN A 70

GAVDAT CV IN CORDIS ET ORGANO

BELOW: *A musical evening in Paris. Each performer sings or plays from his own part book. Music printing flourished in Paris during the sixteenth century and it became possible for several performers to take part in ensemble music. The artist Abraham Bosse titled this work in both Latin—*Auditus—*and French—*L'ouye—THE SENSE OF HEARING. *Freely translated, the text says: "When one considers the infinite sweetness of the sounds of music and their many combinations, it is not without reason that it is said that the harmony of the movement of the heavens gives order to the universe."*

Pulſa placet, digitis miré mihi, lyra peritis.
Cantibus et miris me philomela rapit.
At mihi conceptus numquam jucondior ullus.
Quàm laudes docta qui canit arte meas.

Bosse in et fe

**AVDITVS.
L'OVYE.**

A Bien conſiderer la douceur infinie
Des tons de la Muſique et leurs accords diuers.
Ce n'eſt pas ſans raiſon qu'on diet que l'Harmonie
Du mouvement des Cieux entretient l'Vniuers.
A Paris Chez Mel Tauernier demeurant en l'Iſle du Palais, à la Sphere.

ABOVE, OPPOSITE: *Composers have always delighted in introducing tricks and puzzles into their music. The problem in this canon by the fifteenth-century composer Baude Cordier is to determine the number of voices for which it is written and where, when, at what pitch and in what meter each is to begin.*

BELOW, OPPOSITE: *An anonymous engraving of Josquin Des Pres (1440–1521).*

(1452–1505) who was active in Cambrai, Bruges, Antwerp, and twice in Ferrara, where he died of the plague. He too wrote chiefly church music, including probably twenty-four masses and the first polyphonic *a cappella* setting of The Passion According to St. Matthew. Whereas Ockeghem was something of a mathematician in his art, Obrecht's music is characterized by an element of fantasy and improvisation. He was the music teacher of the great humanist Erasmus of Rotterdam.

The two outstanding masters of the third generation are Josquin Des Pres and Henrich Isaac. Josquin (1440–1521), probably a pupil of Ockeghem (whom he admired greatly), spent many years in Italy at the courts of Milan, Ferrara, Florence, and Modena, and for ten years was with the papal choir in Rome. In his art he combined the styles of his predecessors with Italian influences. He used all the musical devices available and made them subservient to the *meaning* of the words, thus creating an "international style" that had its impact in every corner of Europe. Masses, motets, chansons— his output was voluminous. He was the first composer to whom a whole printed volume was devoted when his masses were published in Venice in 1502 by Ottaviano dei Petrucci. It was the same Petrucci who, one year earlier, had also printed the first music: a collection of polyphonic songs called *Harmonice Musices Odhecaton*. After Petrucci, publishers in Rome, Paris, and Antwerp printed the works of the great composers.

Younger than Josquin but equally international in style was Henrich Isaac (1450– 1517). His early years are shrouded in mystery, but we know that by 1474 he was studying organ in Florence and soon thereafter became organist and music master to the children of Lorenzo the Magnificent, the Florentine ruler and great patron of art. Later Isaac served the German emperor in Vienna, Innsbruck, and Augsburg, and visited Torgau and Constance. He spent his last years again in Florence where he died. He absorbed many influences native to the places of his activity and composed in

those styles. Thus he became very important for the development of music in Germany. His greatest pupil was the Swiss Ludwig Senfl (1488–1543).

A fine master of secular music was Clement Janequin, a Frenchman who died in Paris in 1560 and published more than 275 songs before his death. He took his inspiration from nature; his best known songs are "Chant des Oiseaux" ("Song of the Birds") and "Chasse de Cerf" ("Deer Hunt").

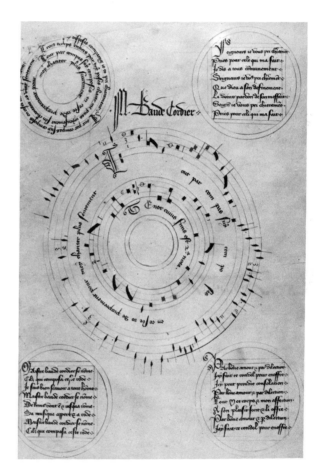

PALESTRINA & HIS TIME

J. Hodgson. Sculp.

You can see how important music had become, how Italy, France, the Netherlands, and England contributed to its development. Masses and secular songs were being written everywhere. Soon a great name appeared, a fixed star in the musical firmament: Giovanni Pierluigi da Palestrina.

He was born in 1525 in Palestrina, a small town near Rome. He began as a choirboy in the church of Santa Maria Maggiore in Rome, and in 1555 became a member of the choir in the Sistine Chapel. After his marriage he was dismissed by Pope Paul IV and became choirmaster at the church of St. John Lateran. He had to live through much intrigue and privation until in 1571 he became choirmaster of St. Peter's. The death of his wife in 1580 made him so miserable that he wanted to give up the world and enter a monastery. But the following year he married the widow of a rich dealer in furs. From then on he had no worries about money and was free to devote all his time to composition. When he died in 1594, he was mourned by all Rome. His life has fascinated biographers and musicians. In 1917 the German composer Hans Pfitzner wrote both the libretto and the music of an opera *Palestrina*, a fictional dramatization of Palestrina's life. Its climax is a scene in which Palestrina is shown as he receives the inspiration for the composition of his masterpiece *Missa Papae Marcelli*. He literally "hears the angels sing" as he composes.

The works of Palestrina are still frequently performed in churches, revealing inspiration, style, and beauty. He is the greatest master of *a cappella* singing which means that voices alone sing, without instrumental accompaniment. Palestrina was not the first to use the *a cappella* style. Flemish musicians had practiced it much earlier. In fact, twelve years *before* Palestrina was born, Raphael had done a painting of St. Cecilia looking upward at a celestial choir of angels with a heap of damaged instruments lying at her feet.

Palestrina was a master of counterpoint (the science and art of combining two or more melodies simultaneously) and of harmony (the combination of two or more different sounds). While in a melodic sequence one tone sounds after another (this is called "horizontal" music), harmony (or "vertical" music) means that two or more tones sound simultaneously. Palestrina knew both, and he reached great power with very simple means. Only an accomplished master can do that. The French composer Gounod, who wrote the famous opera *Faust,* said, "It is the absence of visible means that renders Palestrina's works absolutely inimitable."

We know today that many stories written about Palestrina, "the musical priest of the church," are fiction but the fact remains that he was one of the greatest composers of all time.

Palestrina's most important contemporary was Orlando di Lasso, a native of Burgundy, who was known all over Europe as the "Prince of Musicians." Born in 1532, he spent most of his life in Munich as choirmaster of the court of Bavaria, and there he died in 1594. The Emperor Maximilian II treated him almost as an equal, which was very unusual since musicians were still considered socially inferior. He left almost two thousand works—Italian madrigals, French chansons, German songs, and powerful masses and motets.

The Flemish master Adrian Willaert (1490–1562), who had settled permanently in Venice where he was choirmaster at St. Mark's, was the first to make use of two groups of facing choirs. This style became one of the hallmarks of the Venetian school. He had many Italian pupils, among them Andrea Gabrieli, who was followed by his nephew Giovanni whose compositions for two brass choirs are much loved today. Many composers, especially from Germany, came to Venice to learn the new style. After centuries of dearth, Italy would soon become the most important nation for music.

In Germany, Switzerland, France, and England, the countries of the Reformation, the sixteenth century brought the beginning of a new religious music, different from that of the Catholic mass. Martin Luther, the great Reformer, considered music "a gift from God, and not from men, which causes anger, impurity and other vices to be forgotten." This definition of music remains unsurpassed. Luther wanted the worshippers to take an active part in Protestant church services. This was the origin of the Protestant *choral*—simple and powerful songs to be sung by the worshippers in church. Luther himself was a composer. The hymn "Ein' feste Burg ist unser Gott" ("A mighty fortress is our God") has been attributed to him. But not all reformers were in favor of music. For instance, while Calvin in Geneva permitted the unison singing of the psalms, Swingli in Zurich, Switzerland forbade music in church. In England the Reformation created the *Service,* part of the morning and evening prayer sung in English, and the *Anthem,* the Anglican equivalent of the motet, and similar to the German choral.

OPPOSITE: *Palestrina presenting his Missa Papae Marcelli to Pope Marcellus. This Mass was supposedly written to conform to the standards for church music established by the Council of Trent which was held from 1545 to 1563.*
BELOW: *Cranach's woodcut of Martin Luther (1483–1546). His Reformation movement had a profound effect on the course of music history by emphasizing congregational participation.*

OLD & NEW INSTRUMENTS

Antonio Stradivarius, 1717.

AROUND the fifteenth century certain instruments existed that are still played today. Members of German municipal bands played the trumpet, trombone, and cornett (*Zink*). The mouthpiece of the latter was of brass, the body of wood or ivory. But the most important instruments were those with a keyboard—the clavichord, harpsichord, and especially the organ. In the late fourteenth century some organs already had two keyboards and one set of pedals. There is a difference between the harpsichord and the clavichord though they belong to the same instrument "family." In the clavichord the strings are made to vibrate by little metal tongues that strike from beneath when the keys to which they are attached are depressed. In the harpsichord the strings are plucked by points of quill or hard leather attached to wooden jacks that move in an upward direction when the keys are touched. The harpsichord was called *clavicembalo* in Italy, *Kielflügel* in Germany, and smaller ones were called *epinette* (spinet) and *virginal*.

Among instruments played with a bow, the viols were becoming quite popular. They had the pear shape familiar from our double bass, but came in all sizes. They were held on or between the knees; hence the expression *viola da gamba*. (*Gamba* means "leg" in Italian.) The family of viols consisted of soprano, alto, tenor, and bass viols, somewhat like the family of human voices; there was also a double-bass viol, called *violone*. The sixteenth century marks the appearance of the violin, which is perhaps the greatest wonder among the musical instruments.

No one knows who "invented" the violin. Many experts today consider Andrea Amati, the scion of a patrician family that has been traced back in Cremona to 1007, the creator of the modern violin. Andrea Amati was born there probably in 1535. Some experts claim that Gasparo da Salò from Salo on the Lake of Garda, known as "the father of the Brescia school of violin making," invented the violin. The truth probably is that the modern violin gradually grew out of the older viol between

A series of engravings by Tobias Stimmer. Left to right: (top) shawm; organ; trumpet; (middle) dulcimer; flute; viol (bottom) cornetto; lute; guitar

41

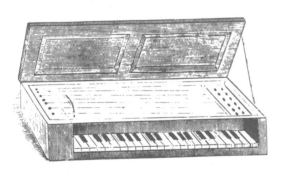

1480 and 1550. No one made them as beautifully as the Cremonese, and Andrea Amati was the first of the great Cremonese masters. He left very few instruments. His sons Antonio and Girolamo (Hieronymus) continued their father's art. One of Girolamo's fourteen children was Niccolò, most famous of the Amatis, who gave us some of the finest violins ever made and became the teacher of Antonio Stradivari, the greatest violin maker of all. The wonder of the violin is that it emerged almost from the beginning in its final, perfect form. Andrea Amati's instruments very closely resemble the masterpieces of Stradivari (1644–1737), and no one has made a finer violin since. From its very beginning the violin combined the quintessence of physical laws with beauty of appearance and perfection of architectural form. It is one of the few things on earth that cannot be improved. Whoever designed the first violin was certainly a genius. No wonder so many would like to have been credited with inventing it. It has been claimed that Leonardo da Vinci made the first violin, and cut the f-holes "to honor his patron," Francis I, King of France. A nice story—but not true.

While the violin was slowly gaining its important position, the older viols were still used. A "chest of viols" was standard equipment in English chamber music until the late seventeenth century. The "chest" housed two pairs of treble, tenor, and bass instruments matched in size and tone. A popular instrument was the lute, on which the strings are plucked, with the body shaped like a mandolin and the fingerboard set at right angles to the neck. The lute was the favorite instrument of the Renaissance. It had been brought to medieval Spain by the Moors from the East where it had existed in different shapes for 3000 years.

As you can see, we know a lot about the instruments and their history but unfortunately not too much about the music that was written for these instruments. The system of instrumental notation used during the Renaissance was called "tablature." It indicated by letters, numbers, and other marks the string, the finger

42

hole, the organ key to be touched; it did not indicate the actual musical notes as our modern notation does. Musical writing varied from one country to the next. Individual composers added to their tablatures their own, often mysterious, personal signs. Almost every important composer had his "code." Experts can translate the tablature into modern notation so that we can play and enjoy this music, but our modern notation does not have all the signs necessary to render the subtle details of execution and interpretation that characterize the music of the Renaissance.

An important part of the lute player's repertoire was the dance music which became very popular in the sixteenth century. Some dances were accompanied by a chorus instead of instruments. This form was called *branle* in France; Shakespeare called it "brangill" or "brawl." Other countries contributed their own local forms to a repertory that was soon to become international. Often the dances came in pairs, consisting of a first slow movement in duple meter followed by a fast one in triple meter. The *pavane* and *galliard* from Spain were of this type, and in Italy the *passamezzo* and *saltarello*. In the seventeenth century many more dances became fashionable, the *allemande* from Germany, the *courante* from France, the *saraband* from Spain, and the *gigue* (jigg) from England. Most of these dance forms appear in the instrumental suites of Purcell, Handel, and Bach.

Besides dances, all countries loved songs and verses set to music. In England the great virtuosi of the virginal were responsible for the golden age of this instrument. The virginal composers wrote music intended specifically for the virginal, and not "suitable for all instruments" as much music was labeled at that time. The *Fitzwilliam Virginal Book* that appeared in 1621 contained the works of William Byrd, John Bull and other well-known musicians of the period. The virginalists developed a virtuoso technique, playing descriptions of storms and hunting scenes, of which the best known is *The*

King's Hunt, attributed to John Bull (1562–1628). It has a realistic chase, including the "Halloo" at the kill. People began to have fun with their music. During banquets music was played by professional performers. For the first time the dilettante, the amateur—a person who plays music only because he loves it—became important in the development of musical art.

PART III
THE BAROQUE AGE

THE BIRTH OF OPERA
& ORATORIO

THE time between 1600 and 1750 was of great importance for the development of music. It preceded the Classical age of music, which remains the greatest era in music. The beginning of the Baroque age, as it is called, saw the birth of opera and oratorio, and of the sonata and the symphony toward the end of the period. The music written during that time is based on the principle of "tonality." That means it was written in major and minor "keys" as is our music today. It was the end of the ideas of the Renaissance. The painters and sculptors and composers of the Renaissance had been dedicated to the Hellenistic ideals of clarity and serenity. You can see this in the paintings of Raphael and hear it in the *a cappella* (voices only) masses of Palestrina.

Now the Baroque became the predominant style in art. The artists began to grasp for regions that no one had ever reached before. The great musician of the early Baroque was Claudio Monteverdi, of whom you will soon read. He too gave up the ideal of serenity and began to struggle with new forms. In his work we hear the suffering of people as we've never heard it before, and also people's joy. Monteverdi was not afraid to interpret people in his music as they really are. And because he succeeded in doing it, he became one of the greatest composers in the history of music.

There are many questions in the early development of music that cannot be answered. We don't know all the answers. But at least we know when opera was born, and where: in Florence, in 1597.

In this art-loving city where there was passionate interest in letters and music, the Camerata Florentina was set up in 1570 as a literary and artistic society. Its members were music-loving noblemen such as Giovanni Bardi, Count of Vernio (1534–1612), in whose house they would meet the singers Jacopo Peri and Giulio Caccini; the musical theoreticians Girolamo Mei and Vincenzo Galilei (the father of the world-famous astronomer), and the poet Ottavio Rinuccini. These men got together to exchange

44

OPPOSITE: *An open-air concert by an unknown Italian painter of the sixteenth-century. The quartet consists of a spinet, a lute, a flute, and a bass viol.* ABOVE: The Concert, *by G. B. Panini. Shown here is a performance of* La Contesa dei Numi *by Leonardo da Vinci, given in Rome on November 27, 1729.*

45

ideas. Galilei seems to have been the leading spirit among them. In 1581 he published a work called *Dialogo della Musica Antica e Moderna*, ("Dialogue on Old and New Music") which became, so-to-speak, the Bible of the young Florentine music lovers.

"Why should words be sung by four or five voices so that they cannot be distinguished when the Ancients aroused strong passions by means of a single voice supported by a lyre?" he asked. "We must renounce counterpoint and different kinds of instruments and return to primitive simplicity." And Caccini, in the preface to his *Nuove Musiche* ("New Music," 1602), wrote, "I conceived the idea of composing a harmonic speech, a sort of music in which a noble restraint was placed on singing in favor of the words." These men devoted to the cult of beauty were carrying on endless discussions about the combination of dramatic poetry and music though they couldn't agree whether the words or the music were more important. Even today there is no agreement on that question, and not so long ago Richard Strauss wrote his opera *Capriccio* which deals exactly with the problem, but Strauss knew better than to solve it. (The truth is that opera

Title page of "Euridice," the first complete opera, published in 1600. The text was by Rinuccini, the music by Caccini and Peri.

to succeed needs both the words *and* the music.)

After Count Bardi left Florence in 1592, the Camerata met at the house of Jacopo Corsi, a gifted amateur poet and musician. There the idea of a *dramma per musica*—a play written especially for music—was created and tried out. The poet Ottavio Rinuccini and the composer Jacopo Peri created what is believed to be the first opera, *Dafne.* It was performed in 1597, and revived the following two years. Unfortunately only the libretto has survived. The two men had even greater success with their second work, *Euridice,* performed on October 6, 1600, before a glittering audience of rulers and artists. Today we know that Rinuccini and Peri had created a new form of art, an early "lyrical drama." It was not yet a masterpiece. The orchestra was small and the composer required that "the accompaniment must not attract the listener's attention." The choral parts were not written in masterly style; after all, both

Opening page of Toccata No. 1 by Froberger. Written in 1694.

46

poet and composer were "amateurs." But the work had an enormous success and it paved the way for the great genius Monteverdi who made the breakthrough to a completely new form of art.

Claudio Monteverdi was born in Cremona in 1567. He entered the service of the Dukes of Mantua at the age of twenty-two as a singer and performer on the viol. By then he had published several books of his compositions and he soon began to show grandiose imagination and wonderful invention. When Alessandro Striggio, Secretary of State of Mantua, wrote a drama *Orfeo*, he asked Monteverdi to write the music for it. In *Orfeo* the orchestra joins actively in the dramatic action and helps to create the mood on the stage. The opera had its first performance on February 22, 1607 at the Palace of the Duke of Mantua. It seems that, for once, an audience realized that it was in the presence of a genius. They cheered Monteverdi.

In 1613 Monteverdi went to Venice where there was great enthusiasm for this new form of musical drama. Operas were usually performed in the court theaters of Florence, Mantua, and Rome for selected audiences of invited guests, but in Venice, a more democratic city-state, a public opera house was opened in 1637, soon to be followed by many more; from then on opera belonged to the people. Anyone could buy a ticket if he had the money and apparently everyone did, for we are told that every parish in Venice had its opera house and that by the end of the seventeenth century over 350 different operas had been performed in 16 theaters. This seems incredible when you realize that the population of Venice was then 150,000. The Venetians were really opera crazy.

In Venice, where he died in 1643, Monteverdi wrote his last two great operas, *Il Ritorno d'Ulisse* (*The Return of Ulysses*) and *L'Incoronazione di Poppea* (*The Coronation of Poppea*). Both works are again being performed today and after more than 300 years they still reveal enormous power and passion: they are true masterpieces in the modern sense of the word. Monteverdi was 75 when he composed *Poppea*

but there is no trace of old age in his art. Like every great artist, he was a genuine revolutionary. He did not ignore traditions but created a new form of musical art that is still loved today. He brought real emotions to the operatic stage —love and hatred, good and evil, jealousy and violence. These are still the major elements of opera.

Of course not all operas produced at that time were works of art on a par with Monteverdi's. His pupil Cavalli wrote 42 operas, which catered mostly to the public taste. He wrote opera for every taste, with tragic and comic elements and plenty of action. Venetian audiences were not very well behaved. A German architect, Herr von Uffenbach, who attended an opera performance in 1715 in SS. Giovanni e Paolo, a luxurious opera house, was astonished when the audience threw potato and orange peels at the artists and even spat at them!

The Venetian stage designers must have been accomplished masters working hard to create

Claudio Monteverdi (1567–1643) has been called by one music historian "the creator of modern music."

47

fantastic effects, such as marine monsters in the waters, deities descending from the skies, flying horses, and mountains that opened to disclose a palace, or possibly a prison. Cavalli's contemporary, Marc' Antonio Cesti (1623–1669) wrote Baroque operas that were monster shows with solo recitatives, choruses, pomp, and extravaganza. His opera *Il Pomo d'Oro* (*The Golden Apple*) was performed in Vienna in 1667. It had over a thousand singers and cost a fortune, but the Imperial Household made up the deficit.

The musical drama was called *opera seria* (serious opera). It was serious but not necessarily tragic; most operas, like Hollywood films, had a happy ending. When the librettists and composers ran out of ideas, they put in a ballet, even if it didn't belong to the story; no one cared. The singers performed vocal acrobatics. Few women were strong enough to perform such feats. The real heroes of the stage were the *castrati*, emasculated young male singers,

with clear soprano or alto voices, who had the powerful lungs and larynx of men. Their influence remained in opera until recent days, and composers have always been fond of writing "trouser roles" for women singing the part of men, as Octavian in Richard Strauss' opera *Rosenkavalier.*

Among the composers of the seventeenth century we must remember Alessandro Stradella (1642–1682) and Alessandro Scarlatti (1660–1725). Both wrote operas, cantatas, and oratorios. Cantatas and oratorios are different from opera: they use no stage settings, and appeal to the imagination of the listeners. The cantata may have many movements, with airs, recitatives, duets, trios, and choruses; it is kept together by the flow of the orchestra's music. The oratorio usually treated a religious theme, but, as we shall see later, Handel, Haydn, and Stravinsky wrote oratorios with non religious themes. The earliest oratorio was sung around 1600 in the prayer house (called *oratorio*, hence the name) of the Church of Santa Maria in Vallicella in Rome founded by St. Philip Neri. They were musical narrations of Biblical stories

in the form of a dialogue. There is a chorus singing the subject in madrigal style and in between there are soloists. Later on, the chorus had other duties—either to reflect the feelings of the listeners, as in the ancient Greek tragedy, or to contribute descriptive effects, to give the mood of a battle or a tempest.

Scarlatti wrote nearly 700 cantatas, over 115 operas and many religious works. He is also the originator of the Italian Overture, first performed around 1685, a composition in three movements (allegro, adagio, allegro) which clearly is the forerunner of the Classical symphony. As a rule every composition had to end with a fast, cheerful movement, leaving the audience in a peppy mood.

The manuscripts and printed scores of the seventeenth century give us only an approximate idea of how the music sounded when it was performed by the great virtuosi. The composers merely indicated the outlines, and the performing artists would embroider the music with "ornaments." Ornamentation is prominent in all Baroque art. The musicians and singers studied "ornamentation" the way people now practice etudes. The prominent singers were able to sing very difficult "coloratura" passages —several fast notes for each syllable of the text. They were also trained in musical composition. Every instrumental soloist was expected to invent complicated ornamentations over the simple melody the composer had written. The orchestra was always supported by a "fundamental" instrument such as keyboard instruments, lutes, or harps. The players had to improvise chords on the bare bass line while string and wind instruments strengthen the overall sound.

The early Baroque created much brilliant music for keyboard instruments, both for the organ and the harpsichord. The great master of the new style was Girolamo Frescobaldi (1583-1644), organist at St. Peter's in Rome. He was famous for his wonderful improvisations; Giuseppe Baini, a noted biographer of the era, reports that audiences of thirty thousand people listened to his playing in St. Peter's. He composed many forms of organ music—toccata, canzone, fantasy, fugue—with inspiration and pathos. Frescobaldi's influence reached into foreign countries, especially into Germany, where his pupils Froberger and Tunder continued his style, which was later brought to unsurpassed heights by the genius of Johann Sebastian Bach.

OPPOSITE, LEFT: *Popular comedy in Italy made extensive use of buffoonery and clowning in conjunction with music.* OPPOSITE, RIGHT: *Alessandro Scarlatti (1660–1725) was the founder of the Neapolitan school of music and a leader in the development of Italian opera.* BELOW: *Girolamo Frescobaldi (1583–1644).*

THE BIRTH OF THE SONATA

Arcangelo Corelli (1653–1713) was a famous virtuoso on the violin and is regarded as the founder of modern violin technique.

THE Baroque age saw not only the birth of opera and oratorio, but also the beginnings of instrumental music. Various musical forms—the sonata, the suite, the concerto grosso—were just emerging. The composers of the seventeenth century were vague in their terminology. They would call a piece "sonata" or "sinfonia" that has no similarity whatsoever to what we now consider a sonata or a symphony. A certain Nicolas à Kempis published "symphonies" for one or two instruments in 1649! Tommaso Antonio Vitali in 1701 called one of his compositions a "concerto di sonate" a concert of sonatas! A "sonata for violin alone" was really performed by *three* people, since the violinist was accompanied by a bass-stringed instrument and a keyboard instrument. On the other hand, Biagio Marini wrote "trios" that were performed by two instruments, namely violin and organ. Biagio called them "trios" because the organist, he said, played two parts—one with each hand, and Bach's organ trios are for one performer who plays the three parts with his hands and feet.

The earliest sonata is in the first book of *Sinfonie e Galliarde* (1607) by Salomone Rossi who was a violinist in the service of the Dukes of Mantua. (We owe a lot to the music-loving Dukes of Mantua; think of Monteverdi.) Of the 27 pieces, 15 have the features of the trio sonata which became the essence of Baroque *musica da camera*, or chamber music.

Musica da camera was music written to be played at home, not in church or at the opera. "Home" doesn't mean an ordinary home but the elegant palace of a wealthy aristocrat or a prince of the Church. Biagio Marini (c. 1595–1665) who wrote chamber music, was perhaps the first professional violin virtuoso among composers. In 1617 he published his Opus 1, the *Affetti Musicali*, a succession of 27 pieces entitled *balletti, sinfonie, sonate, canzoni, arie, brandi, gagliarde, coventi,* "arranged so as to be played on violins, cornettos, or any kind of instrument."

After the middle of the century, the two main forms of composition were the suite (consisting of several dances) and the sonata, which was either a chamber sonata (containing stylized dances) or a church sonata having four movements in slow-fast-slow-fast succession. None of these forms was "invented" by any one man but different composers experimented with the form and created new versions. They wrote compositions that consisted of several movements, usually from three to six, and often some virtuoso passages were added. Twelve years before the birth of Mozart, Veracini wrote in a preface to a book of sonatas: ". . . two or three movements from each sonata, chosen *ad libitum* [as you wish], are enough to make up a sonata of correct proportions."

The greatest composer of the sonata was the celebrated Italian Arcangelo Corelli (1653–1713) from Fusignano near Bologna. He was highly esteemed by Bach who knew his work through his concertos. Corelli's *La Follia* (The Weaver—named after an ancient Portugese and Spanish dance) uses a lovely adagio as a basis for variations. It is often performed. Corelli also was the first real virtuoso and established the violin as an important solo instrument. He is the founder of the so-called classical school of violin playing and his technique is still the basis of all teaching of the violin. He wrote little: two books of "church trios," two of "chamber trios," a book of solo sonatas and one of concertos, but he is immortal. He had no use for cheap effect; he wanted to express with his violin the nuances of the human voice.

Corelli's music has beauty and passion, a fine sense of balance, and the timeless quality of all that is first-rate. His sober, elegant virtuoso passages always express a deeper idea, never deteriorate into mere acrobatics. He created the definitive form of the concerto grosso, which has been called one of the most fascinating products of Baroque orchestral music.

Concerto grosso is a concerto for a group of two or more solo instruments and orchestra. The solo group is a chamber music setting with its own accompaniment. It alternates with the orchestra or plays with it. Corelli's concertos contain a sequence of beautiful dances, wild allegros, serene largos. The eighth of his twelve concertos in Opus 6 is now known as the *Christmas Concerto*. Many great composers were later inspired by his music.

Until well into the eighteenth century the "figured bass," also called *basso continuo* or "thorough bass," was the basis of almost all ensemble music. The "figured bass" can be explained as a sort of musical shorthand. Above or under the single notes of the bass part the composer would print figures which indicated the harmonies he desired. By reading these figures the player would construct his own accompaniment, which left him considerable space and scope. The system was created by the church organists of the sixteenth century who often had to substitute for the choir and arranged the bass parts of vocal compositions with figures so that they knew how to fill out the writing for the lute, the oboe, the organ, and the harpsichord.

Corelli was a contemporary of Antonio Stradivari whose name is synonymous with perfection—and with the greatest violins ever made. Corelli died in 1713 when Stradivari in Cremona was going through his "golden period," making some of his finest instruments. (The late Henry Ford, no violinist, once offered $150,000 for the celebrated "Alard" Stradivari, made in 1715, because he considered it a technical miracle, the purest expression of the laws of physics. He didn't get it.) Yet Stradivari who gave the world the finest string instruments has not even a grave in his hometown, and until a few years ago there wasn't a single Stradivari violin in Cremona. Now they have one in the city hall.

The great Cremonese fiddles also brought an improvement in the violin technique. In 1627 Carlo Farina, an Italian virtuoso active in Saxony, had musical scores printed in which the violinist was asked to play double stops, *pizzicato* (plucking the strings with the finger), *col legno* (with the wooden part of the bow) and *sul ponticello* (close to the bridge, which creates a strange, haunting sound).

THE VIOLIN CONCERTO

LXVII   *Violino*

THE development of violin playing soon led to the development of the solo concerto which superseded the concerto grosso. Probably it was Lully who was the first to introduce the solo concerto in his *Ballet des Muses* in 1666. Then Giuseppe Torelli (1650–1708) began to develop the form of the solo concerto for the violin which still exists today: the concerto begins with an allegro, followed by a slow movement (often an adagio) and closes with another allegro. The same form was also retained in the symphony until Haydn and other composers added a fourth movement, usually a minuet or a scherzo. In music as in mathematics, one development logically leads to the next.

Torelli is not much remembered, but Antonio Vivaldi (1680–1743) is. He was a great composer who enlarged the solo passages of the concerto grosso and made the violin the dominant instrument in the ensemble. Vivaldi spent many years in the service of the Church, teaching at the Conservatory of La Pietà in Venice where he taught violin and conducted the orchestra. He was a restless man, composed operas, conducted in many cities, and wrote some 300 concertos for one or more instruments, for violin, violoncello, recorder, bassoon, mandolin, and others. One must assume that composers in these times either worked longer hours or worked faster than today's composers.

Vivaldi's concertos are beautiful; you may have heard some of them. There is always the right balance between the solo violin and the orchestra, they have beautiful lyrical melodies, and the orchestra contributes dramatic elements. He borrowed from the opera orchestra many fine effects—muted passages, fierce unisons, and tremolos. (Tremolo is the rapid reiteration of a single note [or a chord], an important effect on string instruments, produced by rapid up and down movement of the bow.) Vivaldi's slow movements for the violin sound like songs and sometimes like operatic airs. Bach was so delighted with his work that he arranged a number of Vivaldi's concertos for organ and harpsichord. Bach could do no wrong, but one wonders whether Vivaldi's compositions gain from the

52

absence of the noble violin tone for which they were written, though Bach did a fine job and transcribed these works that might otherwise have remained largely unknown.

During the latter part of the seventeenth century, talented violinists emerged all over Italy. In Venice there was Giovanni Legrenzi and in Bologna, Giovanni Battista Vitali and his son Tommaso, whose *Ciacconna* is still performed. At the beginning of the eighteenth century Pietro Locatelli of Bergamo wrote *L'Arte del Violino* (*The Art of the Violin*) and composed 24 caprices that were a century ahead of their time in technique. Then came Francesco Maria Veracini and the great Giuseppe Tartini of Pirano, who wrote 150 violin concertos and almost as many sonatas. One of them, *The Devil's Trill,* contains the most famous double trills in the entire violin literature. The legend is that Tartini one night had an apparition of the devil who played these devilish trills. The last famous Italian violinist of this period was Giovanni Battista Viotti of Vercelli, a contemporary of Mozart and Beethoven. He was an extremely fine composer whose concertos are now again performed by leading violinists.

OPPOSITE: *A violinist practicing. Note that the seventeenth-century violinist held the instrument at the shoulder rather than under the chin, as is the present-day method.* BELOW, LEFT: *Antonio Vivaldi (1680–1743). A contemporary of Bach, Vivaldi wrote works for the theater and the church. But his fame lies in his superb instrumental music, particularly the concerti grossi and the solo concertos.* BELOW: *Vivaldi's concertos emphasized the interplay between solo instruments and full orchestra.*

THE CONCERT. *A seventeenth-century engraving by the French artist Antoine-Jean Duclos, after a design by St. Aubin, 1765.*

MUSIC IN SEVENTEENTH-CENTURY FRANCE

LET us now take a look at France where Cardinal Mazarin, the powerful Prime Minister of Louis XIV, had encouraged performances by Italian opera companies—perhaps because he was tired of the French Court Ballet. The Italians met with some opposition. They liked to express violent passions on the stage (they still do today), while the French, according to the theoretician Mersenne, liked to "caress the ear" with "perpetual sweetness" (they still do today). But some French musicians began to compose in the new style. The Abbé Pierre Perrin and the organist Robert Cambert (1628–1677) produced in April 1659, in Issy, near Paris, a work they called *Pastorale*, "The First French Comedy with Music Performed in France." They were enormously successful. In 1669 Perrin received a "royal privilege for the establishment of *academies d'opéra*," which granted the right to give musical performances in French, in Paris and the rest of France. The new theater in Paris, called Academie Royale de Musique, was opened in 1671 with *Pomone*, by Perrin and Cambert. It was a smash hit, with 146 performances. Then with *Les Plaisirs de l'Amour* (*The Pleasures of Love*) French opera was definitely established. The great playwright Molière was so impressed by the possibilities of the new lyric theater that he bought "the royal privilege" from Perrin and decided to envelop his comedies with music. Had he lived longer, Molière might have created the first opera buffa. (In 1917, 246 years later, Hugo von Hofmannsthal and Richard Strauss used Molière's play *Le Bourgeois Gentilhomme* [*The Burgher as Nobleman*] for one of their collaborations.)

But the dominating personality of the French musical theater was a Florentine by birth, Jean-Baptiste Lulli, the son of a humble miller who later changed the spelling of his name to Lully to pass as a French nobleman. He had come to France at the age of fourteen, where he studied the violin and composition. In 1652 he became one of the king's violinists and also a prominent courtier and intriguer. He gained the friendship of Louis XIV, and was appointed, in 1653,

56

Court Composer and, in 1661, Superintendent of the King's Music. At the court he met Molière and for ten years furnished music for the comedies of the famous playwright. When he noticed that his friend Molière was becoming interested in opera, Lully began to intrigue against Molière and against Perrin who had been thrown into prison because of his debts. On March 13, 1672, Lully became director of the Opera in Paris. He kept absolute authority over all music in France until his death in 1687.

Many mysteries surround this talented, ambitious man. Perrin died in misery, Cambert was forced to flee to England where he was later mysteriously assassinated, and Molière's troupe was disbanded. But though Lully was a sinister intriguer, a real-estate dealer, and libertine, he also was a brilliant musician. He called his operas *"tragedies lyriques"* (lyrical tragedies). He used melody that follows the rhythm of the French language and created real characters. He preceded Gluck, Verdi, and Wagner in his flair for strong dramatic situations. His orchestra consisted of 24 violins of five different kinds and several flutes, oboes, trumpets, and some kettledrums. And he originated the "French Overture" which consisted of a slow and a fast section, with the slow section repeated at the end.

Unfortunately he tolerated no competition. He persuaded the King to forbid any other theater to employ more than two singers and six violins. Naturally, everybody went to Lully's Opera House. Because of Lully's monopoly, little attention was paid to other prominent composers of his time—Henry Du Mont, Marc-Antoine Charpentier, Michel Renard Delalande. All were called imitators of Lully, but recent research has shown that the "school of Versailles," as it is called, was made of extremely gifted men who had the bad luck to live in the wrong time.

BELOW: *Musicians in a gallery. Attributed to seventeenth-century artist Canuti.*

OPPOSITE: *Jean-Baptiste Lully (1632–1687) originated, organized and monopolized French opera during the last half of the seventeenth century.*

THE GERMAN BAROQUE

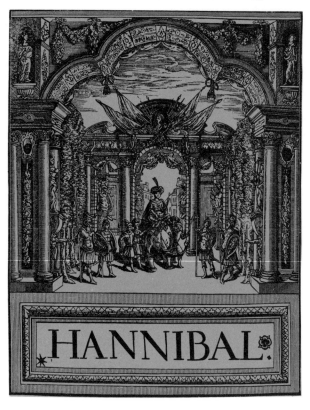

HANNIBAL.

Hans Leo Hassler (1564–1612) was the first German composer to visit Italy; as a young man he studied with Andrea Gabrieli. His many compositions—sacred and secular music, dances, works for organ—show the strong influence of the Venetian school. Michael Praetorius (1571–1621) continued the traditions of Protestant church music, but applied the new ideas that had come from Italy. He also wrote very important treatises on musical theory and instruments which help us today to understand the practices of Baroque music.

The greatest German composer of the time, however, was Heinrich Schütz (1585–1672). He studied with Giovanni Gabrieli in Venice and after Gabrieli's death in 1612 returned to Germany. Two years later the Elector of Saxony appointed him choirmaster at Dresden. In 1628 he visited Venice a second time and met Monteverdi. During the terrible period of the Thirty Years' War he visited Copenhagen three times and served there as court conductor. But he kept going back to Dresden where he died at the age of eighty-seven. Schütz wrote mainly church music: psalms; motets; over 100 *geistliche Konzerte* (spiritual concerts) and *symphoniae sacrae* (sacred symphonies) in the form of cantatas for one or more solo voices with chorus and instrumental accompaniment; three Passions on German versions of the Gospels of St. Luke, St. John, and St. Matthew; a *Story of the Resurrection* which introduced in Germany the oratorio form; the beautiful *Christmas Oratorio* (1664); and his masterpiece *Seven Words from the Cross*.

Like Monteverdi, Schütz wrote some of his greatest works in his old age. Today he is justly known as one of the creative geniuses in music. He was influenced by his Italian training but in his soul he was very German, a great mystic in the spirit of German Protestant church music. His works are frequently performed, revealing depth and drama, nobility and inspiration. He has been compared to Monteverdi because he too was an innovator who searched and found new means of expression.

Two important composers, close contemporaries of Schütz, were Schein and Scheidt. Johann Hermann Schein (1586–1630) wrote sacred and secular music, charming madrigals and one of the first books of dance music for string instruments. He was one of Bach's predecessors as cantor of the Thomasschule in Leipzig. Samuel Scheidt (1587–1654) was trained by Sweelinck in Amsterdam and is remembered for his masterly treatment of the Protestant chorale at the organ, thus beginning a tradition that was to culminate in Bach.

There were many minor masters active in Germany during this century. Froberger and Pachelbel were great organists and wrote lovely suites for harpsichord. The North Germans, such as Tunder, Rosenmüller, and Weckmann are known for their organ works and Protestant church music. Perhaps the greatest among them was Dietrich Buxtehude whose organ music and cantatas were so famous that Bach made a pilgrimage to Lübeck to meet the composer. Bach knew the works of all these masters, but we should not consider them merely stepping stones to a great genius. Their works reveal a lively imagination and a certain seriousness that must have impressed Bach.

The German *lied* had a long tradition by this time. The *lied* is a poem intended for singing and is not the same as the French *chanson*, the Italian *canzona*, or the American song. The typical German *lied* reflects love of nature and romanticism. Isaac, Orlando di Lasso, Hassler, and Schein had excelled in this form; but their compositions, in keeping with the styles of the time, were always written for several voice parts. The Baroque era witnesses the birth of the *lied* for one voice with an accompaniment of figured bass and sometimes an instrumental refrain. The greatest master of this form was Adam Krieger (1634–1666) who freed himself from Italian influence and imbued his songs with depth of feeling. The *lied* was to become a favorite art form with German composers, especially in the nineteenth century.

Schütz wrote the first opera in German (*Dafne*, 1627), but its music is lost. There were other attempts at German opera, but on the whole the scene was dominated by the Italians and their troups. It was not until the advent of Reinhard Keiser (1674–1739) that German opera became significant. In 1702 he took over the theater in Hamburg which had been set up in 1678, and immediately proceeded to go broke. (Keiser was the first of many managers of opera houses who ruined themselves.) Several times he had to leave Hamburg in the middle of the night because his creditors were after him. But somehow he found time to write 116 operas; some of them are now considered quite good. He began by imitating Lully but later developed his own style. His melodic recitatives opened the way for Bach's "arioso." (This form of vocal solo is somewhere between the accompanied recitative and the sung aria. Bach fused aria and the accompanied recitative into the "arioso.")

OPPOSITE: *The title page, showing the first scene, of Reinhard Keiser's opera* Hannibal. BELOW: *Heinrich Schutz was the greatest master of the German Baroque, bringing the Italian choral style to the development of a semidramatic church music that found its culmination in the music of Bach.*

PURCELL

A manuscript by Purcell showing the opening measures of his
Golden Sonata, *1683.*

THE great composers of the Elizabethan age had died earlier in the century, and the minor masters who followed them fell under French and Italian influence. It was left to Henry Purcell to absorb foreign influences and become for a long time to come the last great master of English music.

Purcell was born in London in 1659, and he died in 1695 at the age of thirty-six. His life was only a little longer than Mozart's but also extremely productive. He began as a choirboy at the Chapel Royal and at twenty-one was appointed organist of Westminster Abbey, and there he stayed until his early death. By vocation Purcell was a church composer but he loved the fascination of the stage, and he wrote much incidental music for plays. Purcell's critics demanded an opera. In opera, music expresses dramatic action and people's feelings. Incidental music merely illustrates certain scenes or creates certain moods and there is no singing on the stage. (Much of the music used in the movies is such "incidental music.")

Purcell eventually silenced his critics when he wrote his masterpiece *Dido and Aeneas*, a *real* opera. He doesn't disclaim the foreign influence in his music. His dances betray French elements; his dramatic scenes are reminiscent of Lully's. And he himself expressed his desire to follow "the seriousness and gravity" of Italian music. But he was too great a musician to remain under foreign influence. His melodies, his dramatic ideas, his chamber sonatas and string fantasies are neither French nor Italian; they are simply Purcell. Bach was so impressed by Purcell's greatness that he copied several of Purcell's works, among them a toccata. (Toccata, literally "a piece to be touched," consists of an introduction or prelude, usually a few chords, followed by runs and ornamental figures.) No greater compliment could be paid to a composer than to have been copied by the great Bach!

Purcell has been compared to Monteverdi and Schütz. He was one of the great spirits of his century and one wonders what he might have created had he lived longer.

Henry Purcell (1659–1695) was one of the greatest English composers. He wrote works in all genres: theater, church, chamber, and court.

SCARLATTI, COUPERIN & RAMEAU

Domenico Scarlatti at the harpsichord. A contemporary of Bach and Handel (all were born in 1685), Scarlatti's fame derives largely from his harpsichord sonatas with their bold harmonies and daring modulations.

A HUNDRED years after Frescobaldi, another great master of the harpsichord was born: Domenico Scarlatti—the son of Alessandro Scarlatti. Domenico was born in Naples in 1685, the same year as J. S. Bach and Handel. He traveled much in Italy before he moved to Lisbon and Madrid as harpsichordist to Princess Maria Barbara of Portugal, who later became the Queen of Spain. Scarlatti wrote some operas and sacred music and 555 sonatas for the harpsichord.

Although these sonatas consist only of one movement, they are magnificent in their wealth of invention. Many are so difficult to play that even contemporary virtuosi rarely perform them with the needed mastery—the harmony is so advanced that some modern editors have felt compelled to "soften" it (which is nonsense, of course). Scarlatti expresses many moods in his works; he can be alternately joyful and melancholy, malicious and sarcastic.

The French did not compose the long fugues and preludes, powerful fantasies and toccatas that were written in Italy and Germany. Instead they wrote elegant little pieces in the style of the "rococo" period, with little frills and ornaments; their compositions were compared to a "shower of confetti." They were not written for large audiences but for the elegant ladies and gentlemen in their aristocratic salons. They remind us of the poetic scenes in the paintings of Watteau, of the windmills and shepherds in the pictures of Boucher. It was perhaps not very "important" music, but lovely and graceful and very French.

The greatest clavecinist of rococo art, François Couperin, called the Great (1668–1733), came from an eminent musical family. He was a splendid composer—mostly for the harpsichord —theoretician and teacher, and played the organ at St. Gervais in Paris. Louis XIV raised him to the nobility. Couperin's famous work *L'Art de toucher le clavecin* (The Art of Playing the Harpsichord) is witty, malicious, and scientifically exact. Couperin has been called "the first musical impressionist" because he was able musically to "paint" emotions, landscapes, and "at-

La Danse Bacchique, *an etching by Jacques Gabriel Huguier (1695–1772) after a painting by Watteau.*

ABOVE: *This etching by Giuseppe Vasi is of a performance of the Serenata* Il sogno di Olipia *by Giuseppe di Maja (1698–1772), that took place at the Royal Palace in Naples in 1747.*

OPPOSITE, ABOVE: *A portrait of Jean-Philippe Rameau by J. A. Aved.*

OPPOSITE, BELOW: *Ballets were an important and successful part of Rameau's operas. Here we see a sketch of a Fury from his* Zoroastre.

mosphere.". Many German composers—above all, Bach and Handel—copied Couperin and admired his elegant, Gallic style. And he considerably influenced Claude Debussy, the impressionist master of the nineteenth century.

Another prominent composer of the period was Jean-Marie Leclair who introduced Corelli's serious style of violin playing in France. He was born in Lyons in 1697 and is remembered as the founder of the famous French violin school. His chamber music contains many fugues in the Italian style.

But the French produced a genius who has remained an enigma to this day. He was a profound thinker, a creative artist, and a wonderful performer—and always very French. His name was Jean-Philippe Rameau, and he lived from 1683 to 1764. He was the greatest French musician since Lully.

Rameau once declared that "the text of any newspaper can be set to music." Unfortunately he sometimes used third-class libretti for his operas. As a theoretician, essayist, and composer he got into terrible quarrels with his critics who were still under the influence of Lully. Rameau was a wonderful craftsman who developed the "color of sound" which was later brought to such perfection by Debussy and Ravel. He created much furor with his opera *Les Indes Galantes*, and even more so with the following one, *Dardanus*, which was performed in 1739 and caused violent controversy. The critics complained about the noise of the orchestra, and one wrote that "for three hours the musicians have not even the time to sneeze." Rameau was obviously ahead of his era; in some works of Richard Wagner the musicians have no time to sneeze for five hours. It was difficult for the critics; this was the time of the rococo with its "galant style," and people couldn't understand the first "symphonic dramatist," as Rameau has since been called.

But real greatness always becomes apparent, though sometimes very late. Rameau's contemporaries called him a misanthrope—a hater of mankind—and had no use for him. Today we revere him as the most profound French musi-

cian, a master of logical thinking who has been called "the classic French composer—the marriage of reason and feeling."

BACH: A PHENOMENON

ABOVE: *An engraving by Martin Engelbrecht of a Baroque organ.*
OPPOSITE: *Johann Sebastian Bach (1685–1750)*

J OHANN SEBASTIAN BACH is a human phenomenon who has baffled generations of music lovers, scholars, and critics. Dr. Albert Schweitzer from Lambarene, who was also a great Bach scholar and organist once wrote, "Bach is the end. Nothing comes from him; everything merely leads up to him." Many scholars share Schweitzer's view that Bach was the greatest musical genius who ever lived. But genius is always hard to understand. Bach was "the builder" in music, the architect of big palaces and mighty cathedrals. Yet his musical structures are not cold and lifeless but filled with warmth and feeling. Musically speaking, he combined mathematics with poetry. Naturally, his contemporaries didn't understand him at all. He was too towering, too remote from them: a lonely giant. Only a few composers understood Bach—Mozart, Beethoven, and Mendelssohn, who in 1829 conducted Bach's *St. Matthew Passion* in Berlin 100 years after the first performance in Leipzig. This performance made a tremendous impression and started the movement that led to the foundation of the Bach Society in 1850, a century after Bach's death. Only then did Bach's works begin to be published. Even today we don't yet fully appreciate his greatness.

It is not easy to understand Bach, but I assure you it is well worth trying. In my younger years I was a little afraid of Bach; he seemed overpowering, like a severe mathematics professor, and also, I admit, somewhat monotonous. I've since learned that he is overpowering but certainly not monotonous. Trying to gain access to Bach is like entering a dim, medieval cathedral. At first, you can see nothing except the dark walls; it is cold and quiet and somber inside. But after a while you will notice the light falling in through the painted windows, the outlines become visible, and gradually you become aware that the enormous cathedral is really filled with light and warmth and beauty. You will see the statues of the saints and the mild light of the candles on the altar, and you will feel very much at home there, at peace with yourself. That is exactly what Bach's music achieves: tran-

SKOLNICK

quility and contentment. Herbert von Karajan, the Austrian conductor, remembers how he conducted Bach's *St. John Passion* one day when he was sick and depressed. "I walked out on the platform and raised the baton, and suddenly I stood in a large cathedral filled with music and with a warm light. When it was over and I left the cathedral, I was happy and refreshed."

Johann Sebastian Bach was born on March 21, 1685, in Eisenach, a small town in Thuringia (today Eastern Germany). His father was a

Böhm, one of the finest organists in Germany. At the court chapel of nearby Celle, young Bach studied French and Italian music. At the age of eighteen, he became violinist in the private orchestra of Prince Johann-Ernst of Weimar, but the same year, in 1703, he exchanged his post for that of organist of the new church of Arnstadt. One day he made a pilgrimage to Lübeck to hear the great, old German organist and composer Buxtehude. The meeting was decisive for Bach's life. He was overwhelmed

Morning prayers in the family of J. S. Bach From a painting by Toby E. Rosenthal.

violinist. Bach was the seventh-generation descendant of a family of organists, municipal musicians, and cantors (musical directors in the Protestant church). In the late seventeenth century, members of the Bach family occupied important musical positions in Weimar, Eisenach, and Erfurt. When one Bach died, another would take his place.

Johann Sebastian lost his parents at the age of ten and was brought up by an elder brother, Johann Christoph. He studied music at St. Michael's School in Lüneburg, sang soprano in the choir, and took organ lessons with Georg

by Buxtehude's wisdom and passion, knowledge and imagination, by the old man's fugues, preludes, and chaconnes. When he returned to Arnstadt, he was severely reprimanded for having extended his leave without permission.

In 1707, Bach became organist at St. Blasius's in Mühlhausen. The following year he returned to the Court of Weimar as organist to Duke Wilhelm Ernst. When the regular Court Kapellmeister died in 1717 and Bach was not appointed to take his place, he was so critical of the Prince that the Prince first sent him to prison for a month and then accepted Bach's "resignation," which means he fired him. Bach didn't mind; he was already famous all over Thuringia and Saxony for his improvisations on the organ and much in demand. In 1717 he became court conductor to the Prince of Anhalt at Cöthen. He spent six years there—traveling, composing, and giving concerts. He wrote chamber music and concertos and keyboard pieces, among them the first part of the *Well-Tempered Clavier*. It was a happy period in Bach's life but it ended in tragedy when his wife (and

including Johann Christian, another famous Bach.

In 1722, Johann Kuhnau, the cantor of Thomasschule in Leipzig, died. It was a desirable position but not exactly an easy job. The school had to supply the music for all the churches in the city. The cantor had to carry on involved dealings with the officials of the local university and the *collegium musicum*. He also had to teach Latin grammar to the boys, and do a great many other things. Sunday services lasted

Bach playing for Frederick the Great. From a painting by Hermann Kaulbach.

cousin) Maria Barbara, whom he'd married in Mühlhausen in 1707, died in 1720.

Bach found solace in his work. In 1721 he composed the Brandenburg Concertos, the sonatas and partitas for solo violin, and the sonatas for violin and harpsichord obbligato. Of his seven children, three died in infancy. Among the four who survived were Karl Philipp Emanuel and Wilhelm Friedemann. Probably because of his four children, Bach remarried. His second wife was the singer Anna Magdalena Wülcken whom he married in 1721. They had thirteen more children, of whom six survived,

for hours, and large parts of these services were sung in Latin. The municipal council wanted a "reform" cantor who would modernize the musical part of the service. The application of the famous organist Bach was not favorably received. He was known as a master of counterpoint, a "conservative." But more desirable candidates, among them Telemann, had declined. Councilor Platz told the committee that "since the best musicians are not available, we must select a mediocre one." It is one of the most famous silly statements of all time.

Bach's professional life was not happy in

Leipzig. He had constant quarrels with the rector of the school, the consistory, the university, the municipality. Bach needed more authority and he petitioned the king elector for the title of "court composer," and sent parts of the *B-minor Mass* and several cantatas to the Dresden court. The title was conferred upon him, but too late—for by that time Bach had lost heart in his official work. He could not cope with petty officials, and his students were unable to grasp his teachings. He retired to his home and his family, and composed. His eyesight was failing due to long hours of writing music, and he was quite blind when he died of apoplexy, on July 28, 1750.

Bach's work is immense and I shall only outline its characteristics. One could write a whole encyclopedia about him. Of his instrumental music, many of the organ works—called fugues, preludes, toccatas, choral-preludes—are strongly influenced by the great composers of the German Baroque: Buxtehude, Böhm—their imagination and sense of form, their dramatic vision and tenderness, their melancholy for Italian beauty and deeply German mysticism. All this one finds in Bach.

A prelude for organ in Bach's manuscript.

He is the greatest contrapuntist (writer of counterpoint) of modern times. Counterpoint, from the Latin *contrapunctus*, is the science and art of combining two or more melodies simultaneously. Bach was the master of "free" counterpoint which means he applied all laws and restrictions of contrapuntal writing in free composition. When you listen to Bach, you don't become aware of the laws—but they are there, just the same. Bach's concertos (for organ, harpsichord, and violin) are inspired by the works of Corelli and Vivaldi, whom Bach loved for their melody and *bel canto*—the art of beautiful singing. Bach's sonatas and partitas for violin alone are the greatest violin music ever written. The sonatas consist of different movements; the partitas are based on dance rhythms. Bach's genius erects masterpieces of musical architecture on the foundation of simple melodies. The D-minor partita, for example, begins with an opening allemande, continues with a courante, saraband and gigue, and ends with the glorious

chaconne. It is probably the greatest single piece of music written for the solo violin. All concert violinists attempt to play it but few perform it truly well. So much for Bach's violin music.

He wrote almost 400 chorales which form the nucleus of his religious music. Bach was a deeply religious man, an earnest German Protestant, faithful to the religion which dominated his whole life; he considered his music a sort of religious service. He was not interested in the religious quarrels of his contemporaries; to him

his Protestantism was a positive, living force. His chorales have a deep and universal appeal. He expressed the strong emotions of the crowd in the form of chorales in the *St. John* and *St. Matthew Passions* which he wrote in 1724 and 1729.

Bach's Passions were intended to supplement the services in Holy Week. They are powerful oratorios for solo voices, chorus, organ, and orchestra. Yet they have a translucent simplicity so that they can be understood by the faithful everywhere. There is an astonishing contrast between the choral exclamations of the crowd

("Crucify! Crucify!") and the brutality of the soldiers on one hand, and Christ's divine serenity on the other. This contrast creates an atmosphere of dramatic intensity and makes a performance of the *St. Matthew Passion* an unforgettable event. Somewhat different is the *B-minor Mass*, written for the Elector of Saxony. It is a colossal work, very complex, very difficult to perform, one of the most powerful and yet most sublime masterpieces in the vast repertory of religious music.

Bach wrote five *a cappella* motets which are so difficult that one has always wondered how they could be performed without instruments; apparently the singers in Bach's time were virtuoso performers. Of the 200 cantatas that have survived, one is more beautiful than the next. In Leipzig, where a cantata was sung every Sunday, he composed one for almost every Sunday service for five long years! Bach wrote either harmonically or contrapuntally. He employed larger or smaller orchestras, and often a chorus. Bach did not "invent" the fugue; other composers had written such compositions before him.

But Johann Sebastian Bach wrote greater fugues than anyone else.

The fugue, from the Latin word *fuga* (flight), is one of the most complicated musical forms. It begins with the "exposition," when the "principal subject" (or "theme") is stated alone. Then comes the "answer," an exact transposition of the subject repeated a fifth or fourth above or below. The subject enters as many times as there are parts. Bach also uses double counterpoint (two melodies so designed that each may serve as lower part to the other). He writes magnificent double fugues with two subjects treated in successive sections and finally combined at the end in a stunning climax. Only a great structure—a bold skyscraper, a daring bridge—can be compared with Bach's musical architecture of his fine fugues.

The prominent nineteenth-century German conductor Hans von Bülow called Bach's *The Well-Tempered Clavier,* with its great, complicated yet clear fugues, "the Old Testament of piano music." (He considered Beethoven's piano sonatas the "New Testament.") But Bach's real testament was his last work, *The Art of the Fugue,* which contains fifteen fugues and four canons built out of a simple theme. Bach died after writing the 239th measure in a magnificent triple fugue.

Few of his works were published in his lifetime. He was honored by Frederick the Great in Potsdam in 1747 but spent the last three years of his life in obscurity. One of his pupils, Kirnberger (who once said "He who knows a fugue by Bach knows really only one"), handed his knowledge of Bach's music to his own pupil Karl Zelter who in turn passed it on to Mendelssohn.

Even today Bach is not fully understood. He wrote for the greater glory of God but neither the Protestant nor the Catholic Church use much of his music. He is rarely played in the home. His masterpieces are occasionally performed in the concert hall—exactly the place for which they were *not* written. It will always be difficult to enter the dim cathedral of his creation but those who are unafraid of the special effort will not regret it.

THE GREAT HANDEL

COMPARISONS are always odious but inevitably Bach is compared to his great contemporary George Frideric Handel, born in Halle, Saxony in 1685—what a great year for music that was! —exactly twenty-six days before the birth of Bach in Eisenach, less than a hundred miles away. Yet the two giants couldn't be more different. Bach was a Protestant German who never moved away from his homeland. Handel was a citizen of the world who settled in England to supply the upper classes with operas in the Italian style. Bach was austere, thrifty, a family man; Handel enjoyed life, loved applause, lived in fame and fortune. Bach immersed himself in mystic depth; Handel loved polyphony of Latin clarity. But there was room for both—as there was later for Haydn and Mozart, or for Verdi and Wagner.

Handel was a child prodigy. At the age of four he became interested in music. When he was ten, he played and composed for both the organ and the harpsichord. This didn't please his family. They wanted him to become a solid citizen and to study law. It was no use. In 1703, at the age of eighteen, Handel played in the Hamburg theater orchestra as harpsichordist and also with the second violins. He found time to compose enough music, according to his biographer Mainwaring, "to fill two trunks."

In 1706 he traveled in Italy and met the two Scarlattis and Corelli. With his facile gift he quickly composed several Italian-style operas. In 1710 he returned to Germany where the Elector of Hanover appointed him music director. Still in the same year he visited London where he had such success with an Italian opera that he went back again in 1712 and decided to stay, against the wishes of his patron in Hanover. (When the Elector became King of England in 1714, he must have been delighted to find Handel in London.) In 1726, Handel became a naturalized British subject.

He was England's greatest musician and was very popular there. He loved opera and ran several operatic enterprises, and like some of his predecessors he was in all kinds of trouble and went broke. When he was director of the Royal

Academy of Music he hired two famous prima donnas, Faustina Hasse-Bordoni and Francesca Cuzzoni. The two ladies often got into terrible fights on stage, and on such occasions started a free-for-all among their followers in the public. Handel became so upset that he once pushed Madame Cuzzoni toward the open window of his office and threatened to throw her out.

In 1737 he suffered a paralytic stroke but recovered after a cure in Aix-la-Chapelle. Like Bach, he became totally blind toward the end of his life. Yet he worked, conducted his music and played the organ until eight days before his death on April 14, 1759, surviving Bach by nine years.

Handel left an enormous number of works —41 operas, many anthems, 2 Passions, almost 150 pieces of vocal and instrumental chamber music, 52 concertos and other orchestral works, and several volumes of harpsichord music. But his greatest masterpieces are his oratorios. They are different from Bach's oratorios. Handel was not a devout mystic, but a confident, militant believer in God, the God of the Old Testament. Handel took his subjects from the battles of the Old Testament, the battles of Israel. The people of Israel became, so-to-speak, the predecessors of the English nation, and he celebrated the Kingdom of God in the British Empire. His oratorios are not church compositions, but national dramas expressed in music. Their names recall Biblical history: *Deborah, Athalia, Saul, Israel in Egypt, Samson, Joseph, Belshazzar, Judas Maccabaeus, Joshua, Solomon,* and *Jephta*—gigantic choral tragedies that could be given on the stage. In point of fact, *Jephta* has been a great stage success lately in Germany. Handel used Italian, German, and French sources, but the great choral settings go back to the English traditions of choral singing, of which Purcell was the godfather.

It has been said that the English, who often disliked Handel's Italian operas, admired his oratorios because they recognized themselves in their monumental Biblical choruses. Handel had been able to achieve his monumental impact with a relatively small orchestra and a small chorus. But twenty-five years after his death, his masterpiece *Messiah* was given in Westminster Abbey with 274 singers and 250 instrumentalists. In 1791, over 1000 performers took part; in 1854, over 1600; and in 1859, over 4000. How big and foolish can you get?

Handel's work does not need such proportions. *Messiah* is a beautiful work, very modern, with lyrical arias and powerful hymns, with intense feeling, a contemplation of the life of the Saviour. Romain Rolland the French novelist and critic wrote, "In his ability to speak directly to the people as in many other aspects of his genius, Handel carried on the sturdy tradition of Cavalli and Gluck. But he surpasses them. Only Beethoven has followed in his footsteps."

OPPOSITE: *Handel (standing, right) rehearsing his musicians and singers. Groups of this kind, numbering about fifty performers, presented Handel's dramatic oratorios.* BELOW: *George Frideric Handel (1685–1759).*

73

PART IV
CLASSICS &
ROMANTICS

GLUCK: THE REFORMER

Christoph Willibald Gluck (1714–1787) was born in the Upper Palatinate, studied the violoncello and composition in Prague and in Italy with Giovanni Battista Sammartini (1701–1775). Sammartini has been called one of the founding fathers of the Classical symphony. In his younger years Gluck composed several operas to libretti by Metastasio that followed the Italian fashion. But then he began to travel—to London, Hamburg, Leipzig, Dresden, Copenhagen and eventually to Vienna where he became the great reformer of opera, and as such is universally revered today. In his first important work, *Orfeo ed Euridice* (using the same story of two of the very first operas), Gluck replaced the "secco recitative," punctuated by harpsichord chords, with "recitative accompagnato," where the harmony is sustained by the string orchestra. Orfeo's first aria is not a "da capo aria," but a simple song. Gluck found an excellent poet, Ranieri de Calzabigi, who understood him. In his preface to *Alceste*, Gluck wrote that Calzabigi had "conceived a new form of lyric drama that substituted for flowery descriptions and useless comparisons . . . strong passions and the language of the heart."

Calzabigi called *Alceste* a *tragedia per musica* ("a tragedy expressed in music") and Gluck turned it into a masterpiece of noble simplicity. In the preface he explains:

> I endeavored to reduce music to its proper function, that of seconding poetry by means of the expression of the sentiment . . . without interrupting the action, or weakening it by superfluous ornament.

This is an admirable statement. Gluck "reformed" the lyric theater and created real musical drama. Without him, Mozart and Verdi and Wagner might not have been what they were. Gluck said that "music should be to poetry as bright colors and the skillful handling of light and shade are to a well-designed drawing." And then he utters the famous sentence, "I have done my best to attain beauty through simplicity." That expresses perfectly the meaning of "classicism" in the arts.

Alceste was given in Vienna in 1767 and was a great success. It is still a success. It was followed by *Paride ed Elena* (1770), Gluck's last Italian opera, again with a libretto by Calzabigi. Some of the greatest operas are the happy collaboration of a great composer and a great librettist. Monteverdi had Rinuccini, and later Mozart had da Ponte, Verdi had Boïto, and Richard Strauss had Hofmannsthal.

Gluck was the first composer who understood the unity of poetry and music. He said, "Even the greatest beauties of melody and harmony can appear insufficient if they are employed at the wrong place." No one had expressed the principle of the musical drama better in the preceding two hundred years. Contrary to the prevailing Italian tradition, Gluck tried to be "more a painter and a poet than a musician."

Reformers never have an easy life. When Gluck's works were given at the Paris Opera, after his erstwhile pupil the Dauphine Marie Antoinette had intervened on his behalf, the success was surpassed by the controversy. "People take sides and attack one another as if it were some question of religion," Marie Antoinette wrote to her sister Christine. The quarrel reached its climax when Niccolò Piccini (1728–1800), a popular master of the opera buffa, came to Paris to take part in the anti-Gluck campaign. Piccini was a fine musician but he didn't understand what the quarrel was all about. It was a musical dilettante, the diplomat F. M. Grimm who settled the question. He was always pro-Italian, but after hearing Gluck's *Iphigénie en Tauride* he wrote, "I do not know whether this is song, but perhaps it is much more than that. I forget the opera and find myself in a Greek tragedy." How right he was! The finest operas—I think of Mozart's *Don Giovanni* or Verdi's *Falstaff*—are those that make one forget that they are "operas."

I have mentioned the names of Haydn and Mozart. They represent the "Classical" age, the "golden era" in music. Before getting there, I must tell you about musical schools and composers who created at the time preceding the classics. Many people speak of Bach as a "classical" composer although he lived in the Baroque age. It is not important to "file" composers into certain ages or categories, but it is important to remember that when we listen to music we are, naturally, the product of all music that we have heard in our lives and the music that some of us have played. Our enjoyment of music is based on what we have learned, and know, and feel about music.

ABOVE: *Niccolò Piccini (1728–1800). His arrival in Paris gave critics an opportunity to attack Gluck's proposed operatic reforms.* OPPOSITE: *Christoph Willibald Gluck at the spinet. From a painting by J. S. Duplessis, Paris 1775.* BELOW: *Gluck's reforms of operatic style are most evident in his* Orfeo ed Euridice *where the "secco recitative" is replaced by the more melodic "recitative accompagnato." Here, in Gluck's hand, is the first few measures of the* Finale.

EIGHTEENTH-CENTURY SCHOOLS

CLAUDE GILLOT: Guitar Serenade. *A drawing from the early eighteenth century.*

IN France the early eighteenth century was the era of the *opéra comique*, which has been defined "a work of music in which both the sung and the spoken words have their place." It all started when the actors of the Théâtre de la Foire in Paris got in trouble with both the Paris Opéra and the Comédie Française, the national theater that produced plays without music. The Théâtre de la Foire specialized in the production of "vaudeville" which were simple, satirical songs that often made fun of celebrated operatic airs. When the Comédie Française, through a royal decree, forbade the Théâtre de la Foire "to perform any comedy, colloquy, or dialogue" the actors took their revenge. They suggested that the Paris Opéra should also forbid them to sing, lowered a board on stage with the words and urged the audience to do the singing. The dispute was settled when in 1714 the Théâtre de la Foire was renamed Opéra Comique and became a respectable opera house specializing in the production of certain lighter kinds of opera which were not given at the Paris Opéra. It still exists and performs the same function for which it was originally established.

From France opéra comique spread to England where *The Beggar's Opera*, a clever satire on the conventional Italian opera, was given in London in 1728. John Gay, poet-playwright, wrote the text. John Christopher Pepusch, a Prussian, composed the music. It was—and still is—a worldwide success, extremely witty and amusing, with popular ballads that everybody whistled. In 1731 the Drury Lane Theatre performed *The Devil to Pay*, a ballad farce, by Charles Coffey, a witty Irishman. Later it was translated into German and produced in Berlin in 1743 with the title *Der Teufel ist los!* In Germany, the *Singspiel* became the popular imitation of the English ballad farce. It offered a simple plot, folk songs and good singing without what people called "Italian acrobatics."

Instrumental music too was going through a new stage of development. Many composers wrote sonatas for harpsichord and violin and later for harpsichord or pianoforte alone. The first movement—the sonata movement proper

—formerly was based on a single theme but now contained a "second subject." The invention of the "second subject" is generally attributed to Karl Philipp Emanuel Bach (1714–1788), Johann Sebastian's second son by his first marriage. In addition to his innovation, he created the modern piano style. Both Haydn and Mozart paid tribute to his Prussian and Wurttemberg Sonatas. Some of them are veritable piano scores of symphonies: in music, as I said before, one thing logically leads to another. Even Beethoven's sonatas were influenced by the "dramatic sonatas" of K. P. E. Bach. Like many other fine composers, Bach's gifted son was much admired but rarely performed. He wrote "emotional piano music" better suited for the clavichord than the harpsichord, but his last works were composed for the piano, at that time a rather recent innovation. If you happen to play the piano, you owe a lot to the often forgotten Karl Philipp Emanual Bach.

Sonata form became the dominant principle of most instrumental music. It made possible the great flowing of the early symphony, which was usually of a contrasting nature, songlike and lyrical, if the opening theme was fiery, thus introducing a tension into the movement, which made possible the extended structures of the Classical sonatas, string quartets, and symphonies. All over Europe composers wrote such works—in Italy, Sammartini, Vivaldi, Pergolesi, and Boccherini; but most of the development of the symphony took place in Austria, Bohemia, and Germany. In these countries there was a wealth of composers that can only be compared with the wealth of artists in Renaissance Italy. When we think of the so-called Viennese school, we naturally mean Haydn, Mozart, and Beethoven, but at the same time there were some very good composers around though their names are now forgotten: Georg Matthias Monn, Georg Christoph Wagenseil, Karl Ditters von Dittersdorf, Ignaz Joseph Pleyel. Vienna became the capital of the musical world. Bohemia and Moravia had Franz Ruma, Joseph Mysliweczek, Franz and Georg Benda, Johann Stamitz, Johann Baptist Wanhall. These men emigrated to France, Itaiy, Germany. For a long time Austria "delivered" composers to the world as the Greeks had earlier "delivered" dramatists.

Outside of Austria the most interesting "school" was founded in Mannheim at the court of Duke Carl Theodor. He made Mannheim the center of German cultural life. During the fifty-five years of his reign he spent thirty-five million florins on artistic and scientific institutions. The Duke, himself an able musician, invited a group of gifted composers to his court. This group became known as the Mannheim school. Some of the composers were Johann Stamitz, Franz Xaver Richter, Ignaz Holzbauer, Anton Filz; a later group included Christian Cannabich, Franz Beck, Ernst Eichner, Karl and Anton Stamitz, Wilhelm Cramer. The leader of the school, Johann Stamitz is now considered a very important composer who deeply influenced Beethoven. He trained the best orchestra of the time and introduced many devices which have become standard practice. And thus we have at last arrived at the beginning of the Classical era.

CARL PHILLIP EMANUEL BACH *(1714–1788), J. S. Bach's most famous son, made significant contributions to the development of the sonata and the creation of modern piano style.*

HAYDN: THE GREAT INVENTOR

A watercolor by Balthasar Wigand showing a performance of Haydn's oratorio The Creation *on March 27, 1808.*

OPPOSITE: *Franz Joseph Haydn (1732–1809).*

M UCH of the music mentioned so far has mostly historical significance, and is rarely performed—with the exception, of course, of the great works of Monteverdi, Bach, and Handel and of less famous composers who are now being rediscovered. Most of the music you'll read about from now on is being performed all the time.

We have all heard Haydn's music. In the past thirty years so much of Haydn has been rediscovered that people speak of a veritable "Haydn renaissance." Joseph Haydn is the genius that introduced an era of geniuses. The great German philosopher Immanuel Kant once defined genius as "the talent which gives art its rules." This definition fits Haydn well. He created new worlds of music. In two important fields—the string quartet and the symphony—Haydn started practically from nowhere and developed these forms to perfection.

In the past twenty-five years more of Haydn's music has been performed than was performed during the entire preceding century. Yet Haydn is still the least familiar among the world's great composers. No complete edition of his works exists. The first authentic scores of his last twelve symphonies were only recently printed. Of his operas some are now being published for the first time.

Haydn lived to the age of seventy-seven, composed almost every day and left an astonishing number of works: 104 symphonies, 84 string quartets (the last was discovered as late as 1931), 52 piano sonatas, at least 20 concertos for various instruments, 24 operas and *Singspiele*, 14 masses, 31 trios for piano and strings, and about 175 pieces for baryton (a kind of viol played by Haydn's great patron Prince Nikolaus Esterházy, "the Magnificent.") Yet this list is not complete. Some major works may still be buried in the archives of castles and monasteries in Czechoslovakia, Hungary, and Russia.

The popular myth of "Papa Haydn" as a sweet, doddering patriarch has been dispelled by the discoveries of the past fifty years. We know today that Haydn was a complex per-

Haydn leads his string quartet in a rehearsal at the Esterhazy castle.

sonality with an unsuspected depth of inner feeling. He is always gentle and genial, a genuine Austrian, but this contented gentleman and helpful friend of younger composers was also "a friendly revolutionary" who broke with old traditions and extended the horizons of music.

Haydn was born in 1732 in Rohrau, a village in Lower Austria. His father was a poor farmer. Haydn became a member of the choir of St. Stephen's, the great Viennese cathedral. In those days the noble families liked to have good music in their palatial homes. Young Haydn met an aristocratic music lover, Karl Josef von Fürnberg, who invited him to his estate in the nearby village of Weinzierl. There Haydn wrote his Opus 1, No. 1, now believed to be the world's first string quartet. In 1759, at the age of twenty-seven, he wrote his first symphony. Two years later he became conductor of the court orchestra of Prince Paul Anton Esterházy in Eisenstadt. After the death of the prince he remained with his successor Prince Nikolaus Joseph Esterházy, an aristocrat in mind as well as in birth. Prince Nikolaus built a magnificent castle called "Esterháza" which even the French compared to Versailles. He liked Haydn, and Haydn was devoted to him. But the composer was not happy with his position!

Haydn and his musicians hated "the desert," the icy marshes of Esterháza; they were lonely for the warmth of Eisenstadt and the gaiety of

Vienna. In 1772, Haydn wrote his "Farewell" Symphony, No. 45, and the orchestra played it for the Prince. During the final movement one musician after another blew out the candle on his music rack and tiptoed away until only the first and second violinists were left. The Prince took the gentle hint and gave orders to return to Eisenstadt. "The beautiful and lonely symphony succeeded far better than any letter could have done," writes H. C. Robbins Landon, the eminent Haydn scholar.

Kapellmeister Haydn had to wear the princely household uniform—blue and gold, with white stockings, and was often treated like a lackey. He had to perform two operas and two concerts a week with his court orchestra, rehearse the musicians and coach the singers, and prepare the music for the religious services. Each morning he had to present himself in the Prince's antechamber and ask what His Highness wished him to compose.

In 1790 and 1794 he went to England where he was enthusiastically received. He returned to Vienna a celebrity, the most renowned composer in Europe. As the retainer of another Esterházy, the rather despotic Prince Nikolaus II (a grandson of his erstwhile patron), he was no longer willing to be treated like a servant. Once the Prince walked into a rehearsal and made some critical remarks.

Haydn gave him a cold stare. "That, Your Highness," he said, "is my affair." The Prince left the room, "white with fury."

Haydn had courage and wit. He dared write to the powerful Elector of Cologne on behalf of his pupil Beethoven who would "in time fill the position of one of Europe's greatest composers." Haydn could recognize genius. The letter is a masterpiece of sarcastic innuendo. Haydn openly reprimands the mighty Elector for his stinginess. "Undoubtedly Your Highness has had reasons for choosing to send (Beethoven) into the great world with such a paltry sum." The Elector was not pleased.

The notebooks of Haydn's journeys to England reveal him as a shrewed observer. He was shocked by the local drinking habits and the

"miserable trash" performed at the English opera. As in Vienna, he had many friends, from the Prince of Wales to Mister March, "dentist, coachmaker and dealer in wines." He was interested in everything. On one page he writes about his compositions, and on the next about a recipe "to preserve cream and milk for a long time." He writes that at the beginning of May 1792, Lord Barrymore gave a ball that cost 5000 guineas. He paid 1000 guineas for 1000 peaches and 2000 baskets of gusberes (gooseberries), at 5 shillings a basket. In a cynical mood Haydn observes reports that "If anybody steals £2 he is hanged; but if I trust anybody with £2000 and he carried it off to

Prince Nikolaus Joseph Esterhazy, Haydn's patron. For the Prince's palace at Esterhaz, Haydn had to provide two weekly operatic performances and two formal concerts. While in his service, Haydn wrote more than eighty symphonies, forty-three quartets, numerous divertimenti, clavier works, and nearly all his operas.

the devil, he is acquitted." Once he noted that "Milord Chatam (*sic*), brother of Minister Pitt, was so drunk for three days he couldn't even sign his name, and thus occasioned that Lord Howe couldn't leave London, and together with the whole fleet couldn't sail away."

He worked long and hard on his compositions though you would never think so when you hear the exhilarating freshness of his music. In his later years he would begin right after breakfast, playing the harpsichord to get himself "in the mood." He would sketch until lunch. After a walk he would start work again at four in the afternoon and do most of his scoring. He would work until eight, take another short walk, and compose for one hour before going to bed. It took him a month to write a

mass. He did not know that he was writing masterpieces; he accepted commissions and did the best he could as an artist and a craftsman.

Haydn loved folk melodies and the popular songs of his native land. He often listened to the gypsies from Hungary, to their syncopated rhythms; he often used Hungarian, Croatian or Slavic melodies in the minuets or in the fast movements of his chamber music and symphonies. He wrote with his intellect and with his heart. He was a deeply religious, compassionate man, and he truly believed there would be peace after war and happiness after sorrow. He is the greatest optimist among all composers, and also the friendliest. Haydn believed in happiness, love and life, in the beauty of nature, the sound of laughter, the taste of

Haydn, seated at the cembalo, conducts a performance of his opera The Improvised Meeting—*one of many he was obliged to compose for court festivities. The Esterhazy castle had a private theater with a seating capacity of four*

hundred. Haydn's operas remain the least explored area of his compositions, yet judging from his well-known oratorios he was as much a master at writing for the voice as he was for instruments.

good wine. His music leaves us with an after-taste of cheerfulness. There is often an inner tension in it but it is always resolved into a happy ending. There are moments of deep melancholy in Haydn's music but never the all-pervading gloom of Beethoven. He has an infectious zest for life.

Once an Italian musician feeling very sick walked into St. Michael's Church in Vienna to listen to a Haydn Mass. "I perspired during the Credo, but then my headache went away, and I felt cured mentally and physically," he later wrote.

Haydn himself explained the secret of his music in 1802 in a letter to the members of the Musikverein (Musicians' Society) on the Baltic island of Rügen who had sent him a fan letter. Haydn wrote back,

Often a secret voice whispered to me, "There are so few happy and contented people here below; grief and sorrow are always their lot; perhaps your labors will once be a source from which the care-worn, or the man burdened with affairs, can derive a few moments' rest and refreshment."

It is hard to understand how people for almost a century could have considered Haydn a sort of "second-class Mozart," just as they thought of Mozart merely as a "forerunner" of Beethoven. Each of the three men was a creative artist in his own right. Each is very important in his own way. Mozart and Haydn were friends. The young Mozart admired Haydn and said that he learned from Haydn "how one should write quartets," and he dedicated six of his "famous quartets" to the older friend in deep affection. The Irish singer Michael Kelley, who was in Vienna in the 1780's, mentions in his "Reminiscences" a quartet evening at which "the players were tolerable." The players were Haydn, first violin; the composer Karl Ditters von Dittersdorf, second violin; Mozart, viola; and the composer Jan Baptist Wanhal, cello. It would have been nice to be there.

Haydn called his first string quartets *diverti-menti, cassazioni,* or *notturni.* By modern standards they are rather naïve and simple, being dominated, like most chamber music of the time, by the first violin. But Haydn's ideas were developing. In his Opus 20, written in 1772, he let the four voices participate on equal terms, with the cello singing out the opening theme—something that had never been done before. And from then until his death in 1809, Haydn turned out masterpieces, all rich in invention but each in a different mood, full of beauty and vibrant with feeling. If you play chamber music, you will grow very fond of him. He brought this noble art form—the purest and finest music of all—from birth to full maturity. It is an almost incredible accomplishment for one man.

Haydn has been called the "father of the symphony" which is not quite correct historically. We have seen that the symphony had already gone through many stages of development. But it is correct to state that no one before him had attained such heights in the art of writing symphonies. They are wonderful music—with beautiful melodies, rhythms, syncopations, dynamic contrast, double counterpoint. He could take a simple idea and write a symphony around it. Brahms later said that after Haydn it was "no longer a joke to write symphonies." It has been said that Haydn uses musical instruments as "instruments" while Mozart "sings on them," using them almost as human voices. That doesn't mean, however, that Haydn had no use for voices. Some of his operas have been discovered only in the past few years. The two great oratorios, *The Creation* and *The Seasons,* which he composed late in life, belong to the finest works of this kind; they have great power and tender beauty. Haydn was inspired by his visits to England where the oratorio under Handel had an established popularity. Unspoiled by his mastery and technique, Haydn always kept a popular tone that endears him to people all over the world. We must be grateful for his humor, his love of life. Grateful too for what he gave to Mozart—the greatest musical genius of all.

MOZART: MAGIC & MIRACLE

The Mozart family making music—Leopold, Wolfgang, and Maria Anna.

To me, Mozart is the greatest creative spirit who ever lived. Certainly he is the most comprehensive genius known in music. In his lifetime critics said that his music was "heavy," that it was "lacking in clarity." Even today some people mistakenly think of rococo minuets and powdered wigs when Mozart's music is played.

Mozart is the only composer who could express suffering and agony in beautiful music. He is never the happy optimist that Haydn was; there is an undertone of sorrow in his music even when he is cheerful. He understands that life is made of joy and suffering. He is able to express the human soul as no other musician before or after him could. Goethe, the greatest German writer, considered Mozart "the human incarnation of a divine force of creation." Mozart "lived" music. In 1778, when he was twenty-two, he wrote to his father from Paris, "You know that I am, so to speak, soaked in music, that I am immersed in it all day long, and that I love to plan works, study, and meditate."

The short, unhappy life of Wolfgang Amadeus Mozart is an enigma that we shall never understand. He was born on January 27, 1756, in Salzburg, and he died on December 5, 1791, in Vienna. He was so poor that he was buried in a pauper's grave. What a sad irony that we don't know where the greatest composer of all times is buried! It doesn't matter, however; his music will live as long as there are people on earth. He was only thirty-five years old when he died, but he gave us a world of music. I wouldn't be surprised if the angels in heaven play Mozart as happily as we do.

You may have seen pictures of the little boy Wolfgang sitting at the piano and astonishing the ladies and gentlemen with his virtuosity. Mozart was unusual even as a child prodigy. At the age of eight he not only played the piano, the organ, and the violin well, but had a complete knowledge of composition.

Mozart could compose before he learned to write. In Salzburg, the most "Italian" of Austria's cities, he was surrounded by music. Mozart listened to German, Italian, French

Wolfgang Amadeus Mozart (1756–1791)

As a child prodigy, Mozart toured Europe playing for the royal families. Here he performs for King George III of England.

music, but he never imitated; the music he heard was only the building material out of which he formed his own magic castles.

He was lucky to have a father who was an excellent musician and noted composer, and his son's closest friend. It is not true that he exploited the child. Leopold Mozart presented his son all over Europe (Munich and Vienna in 1762, Paris in 1763, London in 1764, and then Italy), but he always took care of Wolfgang's delicate health, and advised him well. The peregrinations to foreign countries didn't spoil the child's taste. On the contrary. He met great musicians and heard fine orchestras, and he became inspired. In Munich he admired Tomasini, who was later Haydn's concert master; in Ludwigsburg he was carried away when he heard the great Italian violin virtuoso Pietro Nardini;

86

in Mannheim he happily listened to the great ducal orchestra; in Paris he was fascinated by the music of the German composer Johann Schobert. In London, Mozart became acquainted with the work of Johann Christian Bach, Johann Sebastian's youngest son, who loved Italian music and for some time taught Mozart his ideas of beauty, form, and style. You must realize that Wolfgang was then only nine years —and already an accomplished artist.

In December 1769, father and son went to Italy. It was a triumphal tour for the thirteen-year-old artist. He felt happily surrounded by music and musicians, he studied with the old Padre Martini, the greatest teacher of his time, and he became infatuated with the sunny spirit of Italy. It was there that Mozart realized that "passions, whether violent or not, must never be expressed in such a way as to excite disgust, and even in the most terrible situations must never cease to be *music*." Remember these words: they remained Mozart's creed throughout his life. They are the secret of his art. His genius turned every human passion into *beauty and music*.

In Italy, the country of *bel canto*, or beautiful singing, Mozart was fascinated by the most expressive instrument of all, the human voice. Since then, song always dominated Mozart's

Title page of the six string quartets that Mozart dedicated to Haydn—the so-called Haydn Quartets.

musical imagination, and it was no wonder that his dramatic instinct led him toward opera, the wonderland of the voice. His first inspiration came from the *opera seria* in Naples. It taught him much about the art of musical characterization in which he became the great master. After his stay in Italy, Mozart remained for three years in Salzburg in the service of the archbishop, but he didn't like his home town. He hated the narrow-minded Salzburgers who didn't understand him at all and in 1778 began to travel again. He went to Mannheim and Paris and then settled in Vienna where he wrote a German Singspiel, *Die Entführung aus dem Serail* (*The Abduction from the Seraglio*). The heroine is called Constance. After the successful performance in July 1782, Mozart married his own Constance.

In Salzburg young Mozart had admired Michael Haydn, the gifted brother of the great Joseph, but soon after he arrived in Vienna he met Haydn and recognized the genius. Their relationship—Haydn was twenty-four years older—is one of the most endearing chapters in musical history. Haydn, the great master of the quartet, said to Father Mozart after listening to a new quartet by Wolfgang, "I declare to you upon my honor that I consider your son the greatest composer that I know . . ." Mozart learned from Haydn that instruments have a "soul" as people do and that every human feeling can be expressed by musical instruments.

In Vienna, Wolfgang had a busy life. Piano pupils, concerts, composing, the stimulating friendship with Haydn, chamber music evenings, soirees in the house of Baron van Swieten, a distinguished amateur. And always work. When we look over the lists of Mozart's compositions, it seems incredible that any man could have written all these works in the short time of thirty-five years. In Vienna he met Lorenzo da Ponte, an Italian playwright who understood Mozart and arranged Beaumarchais' play *Le Marriage de Figaro* as a libretto. In 1786 *Le Nozze di Figaro* was performed in Vienna, but only nine times. People thought it was "heavy." Today *Figaro* is considered the perfect comic

Mozart at the pianoforte during a musical evening in Vienna.

opera, a masterpiece of which not a single bar should be eliminated. Can you think of anything more beautiful than the overture, the arias of Cherubino, Figaro, the Countess, the enchanting complications, the irony and sadness and the joy? If I should select one opera to take with me on a deserted island, it would be *Figaro* which has all the emotions and, above all, humor. The people of Vienna didn't agree though; they didn't like *Figaro*. But in Prague *Figaro* was a great success and Mozart happily wrote to his father, "Everybody sings the melodies of *Figaro* here."

He was encouraged to compose another opera for Prague. It was rather a difficult period in his life. Most of his children died in infancy. There was no money, and what little he earned was squandered by his wife. Then his beloved father died. And at this time of sorrow Mozart composed *Don Giovanni*, which many people consider his greatest masterpiece. Produced in 1787 in Prague, *Don Giovanni* was a success, but when it was performed in Vienna, it was called "confused and dissonant."

Time was running out, and Mozart must have been aware of it. There is a mood of resignation in many works; he often felt alone with his music. He wrote much and fast, as if he sensed there was not much time left. His symphonies and chamber music became more serene, more beautiful, more transparent than before; it was truly divine music. He wrote the lovely comedy *Cosi Fan Tutte* and his great lyric drama *The Magic Flute* for which the theatrical manager Emanuel Schikaneder wrote the libretto. It gave Mozart a chance of showing the almost incredible range of his genius, from Papageno's folk song to Tamino's Italian arioso to the majestic hymns of the priests. He was trying to finish the score of his *Requiem Mass* when he died. His funeral took place on a rainy, cold day, and the few people dispersed before the coach with the coffin reached the cemetery. The man who has given happiness to millions of people was buried by strangers who thoughtlessly lowered the coffin into a common grave.

A scene from Mozart's opera The Abduction from the Seraglio, *from a performance at the Royal Opera, Drury Lane, London.*

There is no space here to give a survey of Mozart's compositions. (They are numbered, such as K. 515 or K. 516; K. stands for Köchel who was the first cataloguer of Mozart's music.) There is no type of music that Mozart didn't write, and whatever he did, he did superlatively well. One is carried away by his celestial lightness, his sense of beauty, and suddenly by a few haunting moments of doom—such as a few bars in the G-minor symphony, or the last apparition of the Commander in *Don Giovanni*, but even when there is sorrow it is always resolved into beauty at the end. Mozart wants to say that *life is often sad but there is always hope.* He was quite different from Haydn who believed that life was basically beautiful; and from Beethoven who fought against life and against himself, always remaining on earth. Mozart does not stay on earth. In his divine moments, he take us into heaven.

There are many miraculous things about Mozart. Often he uses a simple, even commonplace phrase or melody and turns it into a masterpiece full of life, in perfect form, so timeless and modern that it seems to have been written only yesterday. Consider the range of *Don Giovanni,* which has been compared to the dramas of Shakespeare and to Goethe's *Faust.* "The hopes you placed in the opera," Goethe wrote to Schiller, "you would find fulfilled to a high degree in the recent *Don Giovanni.*" Goethe sensed that if anyone could have composed his *Faust,* it would have been Mozart. He made his Don Giovanni a Faustian character, driven to perdition by his demon.

I hope you will try to penetrate the beauty of Mozart. It makes no difference which way you go—through an instrument, his chamber music, his violin or piano concertos, his symphonies, or his operas. Wherever you go, you will reach Mozart, and Mozart will reach your hearts. There exists no more beautiful music.

BEETHOVEN: THE TITAN

A fragment from the fourth movement of Beethoven's string quartet, opus 135, in the composer's own hand.

OPPOSITE: *Ludwig van Beethoven (1770–1827)*

THE art of music is like a mountain range, with many peaks, and many valleys in between. It is exciting to reach the peak but one cannot stay there forever. Looking out from Mozart across the serene valleys one sees another towering peak: Beethoven. There is an immense contrast between the two peaks although Beethoven was born only fourteen years after Mozart. You understand now why we call this time the "golden era" of music. There were so many giants within the span of a few years.

Ludwig van Beethoven was born in Bonn, on December 15, 1770. His family had lived there since 1733; his father was a mediocre tenor and musician who sang at the chapel of the Prince Elector. Beethoven grew up in Germany at the time of the *Sturm und Drang* movement, which derived its title from a play by Klinger and symbolized the revolution of youth against the old generation and of individualism against convention. It was a sort of spiritual upheaval, strongly influenced by the ideas that led to the French revolution. The young Goethe and the young Schiller wrote some of their finest works in this revolutionary spirit (Goethe's *Werther*, Schiller's fine drama *Kabale und Liebe*). Beethoven was the dominant revolutionary composer. He protested against convention. You may have seen pictures of him. He doesn't walk like the serene Haydn, like the divine Mozart; he runs, with his hands behind his back, through wind and rain, paying no attention to people and events around him, erect and proud. A man whose heart was filled with love for his fellow men and whose soul was filled with the yearning for freedom. There is something eerie about this gigantic spirit who tried to hold thunder and lightning in his fist. One can imagine that Haydn and Mozart often smiled (in Mozart's case it was perhaps with a slight touch of resignation, even melancholy). But Beethoven didn't smile much, though—and this is the miracle—he could be happy, serene, smiling in his music. But no matter what he does he always makes you suffer a little with him. You can't just sit back and close your eyes and

90

relax. Beethoven rarely permits relaxation. He always made it hard for himself, always suffered while he created. Of Mozart it is said that inspiration came so easy to him that he would write down a piece of music, and that was it; you may have heard that he wrote the overture of *Don Giovanni* in Prague only a few hours before the premiere. The ink was still wet on the musicians' parts. But Beethoven continually changed and revised. His notebooks show us that sometimes he sketched a theme for years before it became the final version. One of the arias Leonore sings in the opera *Fidelio* was rewritten eighteen times!

Yet God who loved Mozart must also have loved Beethoven for He gave him the power to move deeply people's hearts. It is useless to speculate whether Beethoven remained a classicist to the end of his life or whether he was heavily influenced by the new mood of romanticism. Beethoven is timeless. He composes with the equipment of the pure classicist, building wonderful, simple, yet great structures. But in his last works he writes music that shocked his contemporaries. Beethoven's five "last" string quartets (Opp. 127, 130–133, 135) are more "modern" than most of the modern music written since. Beethoven did not care whether people understood his music. When he wrote his famous three string quartets of Opus 59 in a new and radical style, and the violinist Radicati, at Beethoven's request, worked out the fingering, Radicati later wrote, "I told (Beethoven) that surely he did not consider these works to be music? Beethoven replied, 'Oh, they are not for you, but for a later age.'" There is no arrogance in this statement —only a creator's innermost belief in his work. In 1824, Prince Nicolas Borissovitch Galitzin, a Russian nobleman and amateur cellist who lived in Vienna and had commissioned Beethoven to write three quartets, wrote to the composer, "Your genius is centuries in advance." Any four string players who have attempted to bring off the late Beethoven quartets will devoutly agree.

There were no rules for Beethoven, except

ABOVE: *Beethoven's expression of his belief in God: "I am that which is./I am all that is, that was, and shall be./No mortal man hath lifted my veil./He is alone by Himself, and to Him alone do all things owe their being."*
LEFT: *The house where Beethoven was born in Bonn, Germany.*
RIGHT: *This anonymous painting, titled* Beethoven's visit to Mozart, *may have been done in Vienna during the summer of 1787 when Beethoven is thought to have studied with Mozart.*

the timeless rules of art and life. He had no use for conventions. His great Ninth Symphony, with its choral finale, created controversies which still exist. Richard Wagner who rarely said anything nice about other composers declared: "A human voice, with the clarity and confidence of speech, makes itself heard above the uproar of the orchestra."

Beethoven made life quite difficult for himself and for his friends. His bad manners shocked the aristocrats who supported him. He fought with his publishers, offended his friends, behaved so unpredictably that his landladies often asked him to move. In Vienna, where he lived from 1792 until his death in 1827, he is said to have moved sixty-nine times. There are still many houses where it says, "Beethoven slept here." He thought nothing of improvising on the piano at two in the morning when he was "in the mood." And when he had no paper, he would write music on the window shutters. If the poor ladies knew how much such a window frame would be worth today!

But Beethoven was no misanthrope. This strange man loves his fellow men in his music as no other composer did before. In his Ninth Symphony he sings Schiller's *Ode to Joy*, "All men become brothers." He never heard this music. In his late twenties he noticed that he was losing his hearing. During the next decade the ailment proved to be incurable. And in his last years he became totally deaf. He had tremendous will power and went on composing. In this period he wrote some of his greatest works, the last piano sonatas, the Ninth Symphony, and the *Missa Solemnis* (his favorite work, as he said), the five great "last" quartets that have been called "absolute music." These works he could never hear with his ears; but he *felt* them; he knew exactly how they would sound.

His whole life was a chain of misery. When he came to Vienna in 1792, because he felt so unhappy in the narrow streets of the German town of Bonn where he was born, he had hoped very much to study with Mozart (who had died

A scene from Beethoven's opera Fidelio.

the year before). He went to take lessons with Haydn but the two didn't get along. Haydn had no patience, and Beethoven was the born antagonist. He couldn't get along with people. He left the old master but didn't want to offend him and secretly took lessons with two experienced musicians, Johann Schenk and Antonio Salieri, and later with Johann Georg Albrechtsberger, an authority on counterpoint. Salieri taught Beethoven the principles of dramatic composition until 1802.

Beethoven was introduced to the music-minded aristocrats of Vienna. He was received as an honored guest in the palaces of the local nobility. They admired him when he played and improvised on the piano. They knew that he was an unusual man and supported him so that he could go on composing.

In 1803 Beethoven, having been thrown out of more rooms, moved into the *Theater an der Wien* to collaborate with Schikaneder, the manager of the theater (who had written the libretto of Mozart's *The Magic Flute*) on an opera. Schikaneder went bankrupt like other opera directors, but Beethoven continued the plan and wrote and composed *Fidelio*, his only opera. It was performed at the Theater an der Wien (where it is still sometimes given by the Vienna State Opera company) and was a resounding flop. People were baffled by the story. Florestan, a Spanish patriot, is in jail, and his wife, Leonore, disguises herself as a man called Fidelio and enters the service of jail warden Rocco to free her husband. The plot is dramatic—there is an exciting scene when Leonore is ordered to dig her beloved husband's grave—but it is not unified. In the early scenes when the jailer's daughter falls in love with Fidelio neither Beethoven nor the audience feel very happy. It's lightweight, as in a German *Singspiel*. But when the chorus of the prisoners appears, Beethoven tells his "message"—an appeal for humanity. Unfortunately the people didn't understand his passionate musical language which was "centuries ahead." Today *Fidelio* is recognized as the apotheosis of man's eternal search for liberty and a woman's faith in her husband.

94

In a moving scene the prisoners are taken from their dark dungeons into the warm sunlight and sing of "*Freiheit!*" (freedom). The same proud spirit of freedom made Beethoven cross out the dedication to Napoleon Bonaparte that he'd originally written in his Third Symphony, the *Eroica*. When Napoleon became an invader and dictator, Beethoven ceased to admire him. It took personal courage to do such a thing in 1809.

He'd begun to compose this symphony in October 1802, when he wrote the *Testament of Heiligenstadt* (so-called after the Viennese suburb where he then lived). It is a letter to his brothers, immensely moving, full of forebodings of his death. Still, he continued to work on the *Eroica*. Beethoven believed that man must meet his fate with courage, that he must find happiness in suffering. His is a dark world—quite different from the bright world of Haydn. Beethoven loved nature, the brooks and woods and meadows. In Heiligenstadt there is still the "Beethoven Gang" (the little street) where he walked all by himself. His *Pastoral Symphony* is nature expressed in musical poetry. Beethoven himself wrote short inscriptions that preface the individual movements, such as "cheerful impressions received upon arriving in the country" or "happy and grateful feelings after the storm." If you love nature, you will understand it better after listening to Beethoven's *Pastoral Symphony*.

Compared to some of his predecessors his output was not overwhelming—besides *Fidelio* and the *Missa Solemnis*, he wrote nine symphonies, 32 piano sonatas, and 17 quartets. But it covers almost the whole range of music. His earliest works reflect the influence of Haydn and Mozart; and in his last quartets, the greatest music he wrote, he reaches the horizon of abstract music—a music that is still not generally understood because it is so gigantic, modern, absolute. Brahms later said that Beethoven submitted to the laws of music "with Spartan rigor" when he wrote these last quartets. Or think of his Fifth Symphony, which is probably the most beautifully concentrated symphony in the whole literature, a miracle of per-

fection, beginning with the famous knock of fate on the door, "ta-ta-ta-*tah*," and developing with incredible force into turmoil which miraculously ceases at the end of the movement. Out of two tones the genius of Beethoven builds a whole new world. He died, after long suffering, on March 26, 1827.

ABOVE: *An artist's conception of the room where Beethoven died.* BELOW: *At the first performance of his Ninth Symphony in 1824, Beethoven's deafness was so acute that he could not hear the applause of the audience. He had to be led to the front to see the clapping hands.*

THE WONDERFUL WORLD OF SCHUBERT

Schubert performs for guests at a musical evening in the home of a wealthy Viennese gentleman.

BEETHOVEN's closest friend and biographer, the Moravian musician Anton Schindler, reports that Beethoven, on his deathbed, said after reading some songs by Schubert, "Truly he has the divine spark." Genius always recognizes genius in others, as we have seen before. That Franz Schubert had "the divine spark," is universally recognized today. You've probably heard quite a few tunes by Schubert without realizing that he wrote them. Some of his songs have become immortal folk songs. His melodies are very popular. A Schubert *lied* is different from any other song; it has a divine inspiration; it will remain alive as long as men sing. What Beethoven did with the symphony, Schubert did with the *lied*.

He admired Beethoven passionately. He couldn't keep up with Beethoven—no one can keep up with a superman—but he walked in his steps, and he expressed the genius of Beethoven in different "romantic" ways. He is called a romanticist because of his charm, inspiration, melodic wealth, his love of color and harmony. But Schubert knows the classic forms of music (as you realize when you hear his *Unfinished Symphony* or his string quartets) and so it doesn't matter whether we call him the classicist of romanticism, or the romanticist of classicism.

Books, operettas, plays, and films have been written about Schubert, showing him as a carefree, easygoing "Bohemian," who never settled down, ran around with his friends, didn't have a worry in his life, and jotted down his immortal songs on his cuffs while sitting in a Viennese coffee house. This is pure nonsense. Schubert may give the impression that work came easily to him because there is the never-ending flow of melodies. But if we listen more carefully to his *lieder*, his symphonies, his somber *Death and the Maiden* quartet, we sense that here was a man driven by deep pathos and passion, who suffered deeply but didn't want others to know it. He was truly a romantic soul who often couldn't cope with brutal life. It is sad to realize that this genius who gave us so much unforgettable melody, died at the age of thirty-one, younger even than Mozart.

96

Franz Schubert was born in Vienna in 1797, five years after Beethoven settled there. His father was a schoolmaster and cellist and played chamber music at home. Everybody played music at home in this city, and young Franz grew up literally surrounded by it. He learned the rudiments of violin playing with his father at home; and the local choirmaster taught him piano, singing and harmony. As a chorister in the Imperial chapel he studied with Salieri (who also taught Beethoven), and for four years he was assistant master in his father's school. At twenty he decided to devote his life to music. Unfortunately he was in bad health, a frail man, and his art brought him no money; he was always in debt. People paid no attention to him. When he wrote to Goethe, whose poems he so admired that he set them to music, the famous bard of Weimar didn't even bother to answer his letters. In the last year of his short life his friends arranged a benefit concert of his compositions which brought him some money. But he suffered from a then incurable disease, and he must have felt it. The wonderful *lieder* cycle *Die Winterreise* (*A Winter's Journey*), is clouded by a deep sense of melancholy. Once more he summoned all his strength and wrote the glorious C-major Symphony. Then he called the famous contrapuntist Simon Sechter and wanted to "take lessons." But it was too late; he died on November 19, 1828. His last wish was to be buried near his admired Beethoven. His wish has been fulfilled: when you come to Vienna's Central Cemetery, you see the graves of the two great composers, and also those of Gluck, Brahms, Johann Strauss, Hugo Wolf, and others.

Schubert was really never appreciated by his contemporaries. They would sing his *lieder* and play his piano pieces but didn't understand his greatness. Like Mozart, Schubert was a darling of the Muses, always blessed with melodic inspiration. A movement of a string quartet, dated 1814, bears the note, "Finished in four and a half hours." His immortal lied *Erlkönig* (after a Goethe poem) was written one afternoon in 1815. Some of the 634 *lieder* that have come down to us are organized in cycles, called *Die schöne Müllerin, Die Winterreise,* and *Schwanengesang.* They are usually performed by great singers at the height of their career. To sing a Schubert *lied,* which is beautiful and seemingly simple, is much harder than to perform a part in an opera. In a *lied* every syllable, every inflection counts, and the singer is not supported by the accompaniment of a powerful orchestra. Many German composers have written beautiful *lieder* but no one attained the sublime art of Schubert. In a Schubert *lied* one doesn't know where the words end and the sounds begin; poetry and music are miraculously woven into artistic unity. The piano "accompaniment" deserves more than this name. Schubert uses the piano the way Mozart uses his orchestra, of equal importance to the singing line. However the best thing that one can say about many Schubert *lieder* is that they are just as beautiful when sung unaccompanied. They are sheer joy to sing.

Schubert was less successful with his operas, *Singspiele* and incidental music (only that for *Rosamunde* has survived). But his symphonies, chamber music, piano, and violin music are performed everywhere. You may have heard the magnificent *Trout* quintet, his last symphony in C major (with its "divine length," as Schumann said), and the *Unfinished Symphony,* which was written in admiration to Beethoven and consists of only two movements. It is not true, as the name seems to indicate, that death interrupted the completion of this symphony. Schubert wrote two more afterwards, one of which has not yet been found.

Franz Schubert
(1797–1828)

OPERA IN GERMANY, FRANCE & ITALY

The opera house in Vienna at the close of the nineteenth century.

CARL MARIA VON WEBER (1786–1826) achieved something that even Mozart and Beethoven, much greater composers, did not do: he wrote a "German" opera. ("My morning and evening prayer is for German opera," Schumann later said.) Weber was fascinated by the romanticism of the stage—the forces of nature, good and evil spirits of water and woodland, sorcerers and fairies. There existed several imitations of *Faust* and *The Magic Flute*. Weber who studied music with his father, an orchestra conductor who traveled with theatrical companies, was caught by the excitement of the stage. He was also a very gifted musician—he studied with Michael Haydn—and at the age of thirteen wrote a "grand romantic opera," *Das stumme Waldmädchen* (*The Forest Maiden*). Later he settled in London where he died. In his last years he wrote the great German operas, *Der Freischütz, Euryanthe,* and *Oberon.* Despite mediocre libretti, Weber's operas are what he wanted them to be—a synthesis of many arts, of words and music, sounds and sights—the very idea which Richard Wagner later perfected. Wagner could hardly have written *Lohengrin* without Weber's *Euryanthe.*

Der Freischütz, a *Singspiel* with spoken dialogue and a rather mediocre libretto, is considered by many Germans as a sort of "national opera," with stirring melodies and nice songs. Until Wagner came along, there was nothing like it in Germany.

In France, where the influence of Gluck was strong, Étienne Nicholas Méhul (1763–1817), who had been encouraged by the aged Gluck, was very successful with his opera *Joseph.* But the most important composer, who is now getting a real revival was Luigi Cherubini (1760–1842) whose operas *Lodoiska* and *Médée* are much admired for their power and craftsmanship; his most popular work was *Les Deux Journées* known in English as *The Water-carrier.* And there was Gasparo Spontini (1774–1851) who came to Paris from Italy and had a triumphant success with his opera *La Vestale,* produced in 1807. Though he was under the influence of Gluck, Spontini showed nobility and

ABOVE: *Carl Maria von Weber (1786–1826)*. BELOW: *A. scene from Weber's opera* Der Freischütz.

great dramatic temperament. *La Vestale* has now been recorded and is popular with the musical avant-garde.

Another Italian composer of this time became so famous that he outshone Mozart, Beethoven, and Schubert. Gioacchino Rossini (1792–1868) was already well known when his *The Barber of Seville* was performed in Rome in 1816. The first night was a flop because the audience couldn't forgive Rossini for treating a story that had earlier been used by the Neapolitan composer Giovanni Paisiello (1740–1816) whose own *Barbiere,* first performed in 1782, had been immensely popular. But Rossini was a man of unusual gifts. He reminds us somewhat of Mozart for his masterful characterization, his knowledge of the stage, his musical wit. It is impossible not to be enchanted by his charm, rhythm, caprice. His *Barber* has been compared to Mozart's *Figaro* and is a masterpiece of the *opera buffa.* Both stories were written by the great French playwright Beaumarchais; *Figaro* is the sequel of the *Barber.* In Rossini's charming opera we first meet old Dr. Bartolo in Seville, Spain, whose niece Rosina falls in love with the dashing Count Almaviva. The pair are brought together by the Count's barber Figaro, a charming and smart operator if there ever was one. In *The Marriage of Figaro* we again meet Count and Countess of Almaviva with Figaro who himself wants to marry Susanna, the Countess's chambermaid, which leads to more complications than a dozen Hollywood comedies.

Rossini's *Barber* with its enchanting music, from the wonderful overture to the very end, was an instantaneous smash hit everywhere—in London, Paris, New York, and Vienna. Afterwards the whole world was at Rossini's feet. When he visited Vienna in 1822, all famous "local" composers were completely ignored. Later Rossini wrote *Cenerentola (Cinderella)* whose charm now delights opera audiences all over the world. In 1828 he wrote the "grand opera" *Le Comte Ory.* It was written for the vast stage of the Paris Opéra where Daniel-Esprit Auber had just had a sensational success with *La Muette de Portici,* a work full of theatrical effects and stunts—there was even an eruption of Vesuvius on the stage—with elaborate settings, lavish ballets that had no connection with the plot, and a lot of brassy effects in the orchestra.

In this "grand opera" style Rossini wrote *William Tell*, a sort of early historical technicolor opera but Rossini, a great master, did it so well that it has survived to this day. The overture alone is worth the admission. All in all he wrote 38 operas; he did a new one every six months. After the premier of *William Tell* in 1829 something strange happened: Rossini, at the age of thirty-seven, gave up composing. He lived thirty-nine years longer but produced nothing except a *Stabat* and a *Mass*. There are two explanations. One is that he was so lazy and had so much money that he didn't need to work any longer. The other is that he was so impressed by the work of Giacomo Meyerbeer, the master of the "grand opera," that Rossini thought he was no longer needed. Rossini knew the secret of when to stop—which is always hard when you eat well or when you are successful. And he loved to eat well. He settled near Paris and lived the life of a happy epicurean. Many great dishes are now called after him, "Tournedos Rossini."

At the time when Rossini gave up writing opera, two other Italians became, and still are, famous. Gaetano Donizetti (1797–1848) wrote 71 operas, and much sacred and instrumental music. He worked with incredible facility. A story goes that his masterpiece *Don Pasquale*, which is still in the repertory of many opera houses, was written in ten days! When somebody told him that Rossini had needed thirteen days to write his *Barber of Seville*, Donizetti said, "Rossini was always a slow worker." Other Donizetti operas are *L'Elisir d'Amore, Lucia di Lammermoor, La Fille du Regiment, La Favorite*. He had a fine sense of both tragedy and comedy, and a dramatic instinct that was never surpassed by anyone until Verdi came along. Donizetti has an elegant style and he developed the art of *bel canto* which makes the voice the principal instrument of emotion. His

ABOVE: *Giacchino Rossini (1792–1868) reached the height of his career early in life. He stopped composing for the stage at the age of thirty-seven, but to the end of his life his home was the center of the artistic world in Paris.*
BELOW: *A scene from Rossini's best-known opera* William Tell.

arias are incredibly difficult to sing, beautiful melodies enriched with artistic thrills. No wonder that the great prima donnas since his days have founded their fame on singing the title role in *Lucia di Lammermoor*.

The purest exponent of the art of *bel canto* opera was Vincenzo Bellini (1801–1835). He also died young but he won great fame by his art, his melodies, and his dramatic sense. Right now there is a great Bellini renaissance and his three masterpieces *Norma*, *La Sonnambula* (*The Sleep Walker*) and *I Puritani* have been "rediscovered." No wonder. With superlative performers such as Maria Callas, Bellini's operas have become stunning masterpieces of exciting Italian opera. The vocal demands are terrific. The role of Norma is considered one of the most difficult of all soprano parts. Any performer who can sing well in *Norma* becomes a star of the first magnitude. Modern prima donnas love the challenge. Had Bellini lived longer, he might have become one of the greatest composers of his century.

ABOVE: *Gaetano Donizetti (1797–1848)*.
BELOW: *A scene from Donizetti's opera* Lucia di Lammermoor.
LEFT: *A scene from Vincenzo Bellini's opera* Norma.

101

GRAND OPERA

IT is no accident that Spontini, Rossini, Donizetti, and Bellini produced their best works in Paris, where a night at the opera was then a brilliant event. The French capital had developed its own operatic style which even Wagner acknowledged when he wrote in 1865 to King Ludwig II of Bavaria, "The style of the Paris school is still the dominating influence on the taste of almost every nation. . . . In Paris, Italians and Germans immediately become French."

We have mentioned earlier the French *opéra comique* whose master, François-Adrien Boieldieu (1775–1834), wrote some fine operas, such as *The Caliph of Baghdad, Jean de Paris,* and *La Dame Blanche.* (Perhaps the best-known musical piece of this time was written by an amateur musician and soldier, Rouget de l'Isle, who in 1792 created France's *Marseillaise,* the finest national anthem ever written.) But the French style soon degenerated into the empty spectacle of the "grand opera," an extravaganza of noise and action, choruses and dances.

The most famous composer of the French "grand opera" was, paradoxically, a Jew from Berlin named Jakob Beer who went to Paris and became world-famous as Giacomo Meyerbeer (1791–1864). An extremely gifted musician and a smart showman as well, he decided to give the people what they wanted and created a grand show with rich costumes, demons and phantoms, councils and processions, and gun blasts. The French loved him; Balzac called his opera *Les Huguénots* "as true as history itself"; the critics raved. Elsewhere Meyerbeer was less admired. Mendelssohn called the ballet in *Robert le Diable (Robert the Devil)* "a scandal." It was danced by nuns who had come out of their graves at midnight to amuse themselves in the ruins of a monastery! Schumann wrote about Meyerbeer's "monstrosities," and Wagner called his music "effect without cause or reason." But while Meyerbeer was perhaps overestimated in France, he is now unjustly belittled. He was a great master of orchestration and had an unfailing instinct for the stage; even Wagner admitted that the love scene in the second act of *Les Huguenots* was one of the finest ever written. The libretti for his most successful operas were written by Eugene Scribe (1791–1861), a master librettist who developed the writing of opera into a real art. He was able to insert effective arias at the most improbable moments of the plot. Auguste, the famous *claque chef* (cheer leader) of the Paris Opéra who would "arrange" for applause and ovation in return for a substantial reward, used to say that every aria of Scribe "could be made"—meaning that he could start a salvo of applause after such an aria without breaking up the flow of action. Other masters of the "grand opera" style were Jacques Halévy (*La Juive*), Ferdinand Herold (*Zampa*), and Adolphe Adam (called "the French Weber") who composed *Si j'étais Roi* (*If I Were King*), *The Postillon of Long-jumeau*, and the indestructible ballet score *Giselle*.

Grand opera soon created a healthy reaction. Wagner, Verdi, and later Debussy, worked against the emptiness of this kind of spectacle.

ABOVE: *This humorous drawing by Honoré Daumier is titled* THE ORCHESTRA DURING THE PERFORMANCE OF A TRAGEDY. *Judging from the expression of the musicians, the tragedy being performed was not as gripping as the composer perhaps intended.*
OPPOSITE: *Giacomo Meyerbeer (1791–1864), a German, became the leading composer of French grand opera.* LEFT: *A scene from Meyerbeer's opera* The Prophet.

THE ROMANTICISTS

Frédéric Chopin (1810–1839). A portrait by Delacroix (1798–1863).

WHILE the grand opera fascinated its addicts in Paris, there began in neighboring Germany the era of "romanticism," which originated in the field of literature, and in music is represented by Mendelssohn, Schumann, Chopin, Liszt, and (in France) by Berlioz. The romanticists moved away from the gigantic force of Beethoven's symphonies; they loved music of a poetic nature, sentimental moods, and lyric unity. But let us not think of "moonlight romanticism" and such sentimental nonsense. The romanticists were great masters who knew their art well and wrote beautifully, though perhaps not for everybody. "I should not like to be understood by everybody," Schumann once said.

Felix Mendelssohn-Bartholdy (1809–1847) was the grandson of the great Jewish philosopher Moses Mendelssohn, and the son of a wealthy banker in Berlin. The Mendelssohns had for generations been patrons of literature and the arts. Immensely gifted, Mendelssohn was only seventeen when he wrote the transparently beautiful, enchanting overture to Shakespeare's *A Midsummer Night's Dream*, and became world-famous. He rediscovered the works of Johann Sebastian Bach, conducting in 1829 a performance of the master's *St. Matthew Passion*, and founded the famous Conservatory in Leipzig. Mendelssohn is universally beloved as the composer of five symphonies (the best known are the *Italian* and the *Scottish* symphonies), of the poetic, intimate piano pieces called *Songs without Words*, of fine overtures (*Hebrides*), and of a beautiful violin concerto which every great violinist has performed—a work of tender poetry and eternal youth. And Mendelssohn was an inspiration for his greatest admirer, Robert Schumann (1810–1856).

Schumann, like all romantic composers, was devoted both to music and literature. He loved Goethe, Jean Paul, and Byron, and while he composed piano pieces, he also wrote poetry. He was romantic and sentimental, a dreamer with many gifts. In 1840 he married Clara Wieck, the daughter of his first piano teacher, herself a musician of distinction and a talented pianist. Schumann had dreamed of a career as a concert pianist but his right hand was partly paralyzed. After his marriage he had a few happy years, writing fine symphonies, choral works, piano works, and chamber music. But he began to suffer from attacks of depression (which became evident in the melancholy moments of his music) and gradually his mind became deranged. After an attempt to drown himself, he had to be interned in an asylum until death came, mercifully, in 1856.

Schumann is much loved now. We understand his love of darkness and night, his complicated rhythms, his powerful climaxes. He wrote beautiful *lieder* (some in cycles, such as *Dichterliebe, Frauenliebe und -leben*) and he inspired many great musicians who came after him, especially Wagner.

One of Schumann's heroes was Frédéric Chopin (1810–1849), son of a French father and a Polish mother. (Both nations claim Chopin and we must not blame them. The French pronounce his name in French, while the Poles call him "*Shop*-pen.") Musicians everywhere are fascinated by the beautiful music of this romantic genius. He first astonished the world as a child prodigy on the piano. After a triumphal European concert tour Chopin decided to live, like many Polish émigrés, in Paris, where he became the idol of the aristocratic society, and a brilliant performer. His romance with the poet George Sand (the pseudonym of Amandine Aurore Lucie Dupin), the most famous French woman of his time, is known from books and films. Chopin was certainly a great composer, very different from the classicists. His art was directed toward the piano, for which he created a very personal style, with a harmonic system so much his own that one immediately recognizes a Chopin composition. Listening to his preludes, nocturnes, etudes and fantasies one thinks of beautiful ladies in elegant salons, of candlelight and young lovers. But Chopin was not only the master of the elegant, nostalgic, tender piece; he also wrote some exciting melodies, rousing the revolutionary spirit of Poland. So strongly do the Poles feel about their national

Felix Mendelssohn-Bartholdy (1809–1847).

Robert Schumann. (1810–1856). A lithograph by Kriehuber, 1839.

105

hero that during World War II, when Poland was under brutal German domination, the Polish patriots would secretly meet in the cellars of the bombed-out houses in Warsaw, not to plot against the Germans (that seemed hopeless), but to listen to the revolutionary sounds of their beloved Chopin. (His *Revolutionary Etude* became a sort of secret national anthem in Poland.) The Germans had forbidden the playing of his music and punished people who listened to it. They couldn't have payed Chopin a greater compliment. It proves again that music does more to rouse the spirit of people than any other art. Chopin's music is pure magic when it is performed by a great Polish pianist such as Artur Rubinstein.

What Chopin did for the piano the Italian Niccolò Paganini (1782–1840), the greatest violin virtuoso of all time, did for his instrument. His incredible accomplishments are still a source of wonderment to violinists everywhere. His life is surrounded by many legends. One night in Leghorn he gambled away everything he had, including his lovely Amati violin. A wealthy French music lover named Livron lent him a Guarneri for his concert the next day. Paganini played it so beautifully that Livron, overcome with emotion, gave him the Guarneri asking that he must never let anyone else play it. Paganini called his powerful Guarneri his "cannon" and after his death bequeathed it to his native city, Genoa, where it is now exhibited under glass in the City Hall.

Paganini made a demoniac impression on his audiences. Schubert attended a Paganini concert in Vienna and afterwards was "as in trance." Chopin was "overcome with emotion" when he heard Paganini in Warsaw, and made piano transcriptions from Paganini's Second Violin Concerto. Schumann wrote: "Paganini's compositions contain the purest and most valuable qualities," and made piano transcriptions of twelve Paganini caprices. Brahms published variations on the last caprice; Liszt also transcribed his caprices. Today Paganini is admired as a great composer; you will hear the demoniac undertones and the magic mood in his violin compositions. Unfortunately they are so difficult that only the virtuosi can play them as they should be played. Paganini advanced the technique of the violin more than any previous performer; he had an exceptionally good ear and could perform with perfect intonation on a fiddle whose strings were out of tune.

The romantic era was the time of romantic virtuosi. The Hungarian Franz Liszt (1811–1886) began in the usual style as a child prodigy and became a much admired pianist, but at the age of thirty-six he gave up a brilliant career and devoted himself to composition. In 1848, a fateful year in Europe, Liszt went to Weimar where he spent twelve years composing, teaching and conducting. In his piano compositions (hundreds of them) he revolutionized the technique of the instrument. In the works of Liszt the piano begins to sound like an orchestra, with rich tone colors and much power. Like all romanticists, Liszt believed in virtuosity and improvisation which came close to the romantic ideal of "instantaneous creation." (Paganini freely improvised during his concerts; Chopin spent heavenly hours improvising on the piano; too bad they didn't have tape recorders at that time.) In one of his compositions Liszt uses one chord which he develops, deriving melody and accompaniment, presenting the same chord slowly and then again fast, writing ornamentations around it. No wonder people were astonished. One of the slogans of the romanticists was "*épater les bourgeois*"—"to shock the philistines." Liszt succeeded admirably.

From the keyboard Liszt proceeded to the orchestra which gave him greater expression and scope. He developed the idea of "program music" from the words with which Beethoven had prefaced his Sixth Symphony: "*Pastoral Symphony*—no musical picture, just a piece of music that expresses the feeling that one has when enjoying country life." Liszt did not write up a "program" after which he composed music; he explained his idea as follows: "The musician who is inspired by nature, exhales in tones nature's most tender secrets without copying it." That was what Liszt did when he began to write

his famous "symphonic poems."

"The composer of instrumental music, by virtue of the nobility of sentiment and the grandeur of form, is well able to mount to greater heights than any other," Liszt once wrote, and he proved it with his *Faust Symphony* (1857). It impressed Richard Wagner who wanted to write his own "Faust Symphony" but wrote only a *Faust Overture*. Liszt was a generous man and a helpful friend who did much to promote the music of Wagner, Schumann, Smetana, César Franck, and Berlioz.

The greatness of Hector Berlioz (1803–1869) was firmly established in our century. His contemporaries couldn't agree on him. He had his own unconventional style which shocked many people. He had triumphs and failures, tempestuous love affairs, many friends and more enemies. He was a gifted writer with caustic wit and he wrote what he thought. This didn't please many people. "Musicians are alarmed at the liberties he takes with harmony, and his go-to-the-devil style," wrote another great Frenchman, Claude Debussy. Berlioz loves strange, shocking subjects and he turns them into powerful, often shocking music. If you've heard his "Witches Sabbath" and "March to the Gallows" in the *Fantastic Symphony*, you will certainly be deeply impressed. One may not love his music but one is touched by its power. He is a master of expression—he can say things in music from tender whispers to brutal shouts. The best of his nine overtures, *Roman Carnival*, his opera *Benvenuto Cellini*, his orchestral work *Harold in Italy*, his dramatic symphony *Romeo and Juliet* and his oratorio *The Damnation of Faust* are works of great force. In *Harold* he wrote a magnificent solo part for the viola (which is the larger brother of the violin) for Paganini who wanted to try out a Stradivari viola. Unfortunately Paganini didn't like the piece "because it contains too many rests." Virtuosi like to be heard all the time! Berlioz called his symphonies "instrumental dramas" or "dramas without voices," choosing wild, heroic, horrifying subjects. Today we know that he helped to create modern orchestral technique.

ABOVE: *A caricature study of Liszt playing the piano.*
BELOW: *Hector Berlioz (1803–1869), the leading exponent of French romantic music.*

WAGNER: CONTROVERSIAL GENIUS

A *page from Wagner's* Die Meistersinger von Nürnberg *(1862–1867).*

No composer has been more praised and maligned, more admired and cursed than Richard Wagner, who was born in Leipzig in 1813. Even today people don't agree about him. To the "Wagnerians" he is a godlike figure: to the "anti-Wagnerians" he represents all that is bad in art—exaggerated sentimentality and monumental boredom. The truth is perhaps that Wagner is a little of everything. But no matter how one feels about his work, one cannot deny that he was a genius and that no musician has exerted a similar influence on all musicians who came after him.

Wagner was an extraordinary artist who led an extraordinary life. He didn't start as a musician but as a poet and dramatist. He was eighteen when he began to study counterpoint, after taking a few piano and violin lessons. And all the time he was interested in philosophy. He worked as conductor at theaters in Würzburg, Magdeburg, Königsberg, and Riga, and then he moved to Paris. There he finished *Rienzi,* a work in the French "grand opera" style—with ballets, trumpets and sword dances but rarely performed today. But then he started to work on *The Flying Dutchman,* "with which," he said, "I escaped from all the mist of instrumental music into the clearness of drama." It is the dramatic legend of the captain of a ghost ship who is damned to sail the seas until he is redeemed by the love of a woman. It is a fine story and Wagner makes the most of it; his Dutchman is the eternal Ahasuerus, the Wandering Jew, always hunted—until he finds Senta.

In 1843 Wagner became court kapellmeister in Dresden, and there *Tannhäuser* had its first performance in 1845. This opera still has arias, prayers, entrances, and big choruses in the style of the despised Meyerbeer, but there are also entirely new moments of musical drama. In 1849 Wagner had to run away from Dresden after he fought on the barricades side by side with the revolutionaries. (Wagner was rarely "for" something, almost always "against"—a great protester.) He found refuge with Liszt in Weimar, and from there he went to Switzerland. He lived in exile until his return to Germany in 1864, under the benevolent protection of the Bavarian King Ludwig II. The following year one of his masterpieces, *Tristan and Isolde*, was performed in Munich under Hans von Bülow, the celebrated German conductor and wit. Wagner was now recognized as a great composer but he was still in trouble. He offended everybody. His finances were chaotic; he always spent more money than he made.

At last, he was forced to leave Bavaria (where, it was said, he had too much influence on the somewhat mentally unbalanced king), and he went to Triebschen, near Lucerne, Switzerland, and married Cosima, the former wife of Hans von Bülow and the daughter of Liszt. In 1871 the aging revolutionary watched with pride the birth of the new German empire. He composed an *Imperial March* for the occasion. It was time to return to Germany, and to build himself a monument that would endure—a temple where his works could be performed, for he had often said that they could not be played in conventional opera houses.

On May 22, 1872, the cornerstone was laid on the Green Hill in the small town of Bayreuth, where the city fathers had given Wagner a site for his future Festspielhaus. For the occasion, Wagner conducted the Ninth Symphony of the venerated Beethoven. Four years later he opened the festival theater that he had designed, down to all the acoustic details. The first Bayreuth Festival was a great artistic success but a financial failure. It ended with a deficit of 150,000 marks. But Wagner's fame was now immortal. He wrote his last work, the monumental *Parsifal*, and died of a heart attack in his beloved Venice, in the Vendramin Palace overlooking the Grand Canal, on February 13, 1883, while writing an essay. The last two words he put down were "*Liebe-Tragik.*" That means "love-tragic" and sums up his whole art.

Wagner is a problematic genius. I am not sure at all how you will feel about his works. There is very little disagreement among music lovers about Haydn or Mozart, or about Schubert or Verdi. But just mention Richard Wagner and there will be wild arguments. Other composers

Richard Wagner (1813–1883), genius of romantic opera.

wrote operas that lasted two or three hours. Wagner wrote operas that lasted for five hours. At the Bayreuth Festival they begin at four in the afternoon, and last, with long intermissions for food and drink, until eleven at night! Let me tell you my own experience with Wagner's work. As a young boy I was fascinated by his early works, the romantic *Lohengrin*, the exciting *Tannhäuser*. Later I was deeply moved by the heroic and lyric tragedy of *Tristan and Isolde*, and the magnificent humor in *Meistersinger*. And today I love certain parts of the *Ring*, particularly *Rheingold* and the first act of *Götterdämmerung* (*Twilight of the Gods*) and parts of *Parsifal*. I also like the beginning of the *Flying Dutchman*. It is almost impossible to sit through a whole evening of Wagner, except in Bayreuth, where the excitement for the eyes is the same as for the ears. Everything in Wagner's work takes on grandiose, heroic proportions—his gods and goddesses, his love scenes, his hatred and glorification. There are magnificent moments in *Tristan* and in *Walküre*—but also moments of boredom. The Bayreuth Fest-

spielhaus has the best acoustics in the world and also the most uncomfortable seats. No wonder, since the seats were designed to help the acoustics. Wagner thoroughly understood the mysterious science of acoustics. He invented the "covered" orchestra pit. The brass section sits all the way back underneath the stage. The effect is a wonderful blend of all sections of the orchestra; the music comes through with almost crystal-clear transparency. In most opera houses the audience is shocked by the brassy effects of Wagner's score; in Bayreuth the music sounds mellow and beautiful.

Richard Wagner's great contribution to music is the creation of a new style, known as the *Gesamtkunstwerk*, or "total work of art," in which poetry and music, drama and scenery, lights and sound, singing and acting, are blended into an exciting unity. In his late masterpieces—*Tristan*, *Meistersinger*, and the "tetralogy" (four works forming a unit) *Ring des Nibelungen* with its four evenings, *Rheingold*, *Walküre*, *Siegfried* and *Götterdämmerung*, and his final work, *Parsifal*—he no longer wrote

Scenes from Wagner's operas. BOTTOM: *Siegfried and Brunhilde in* Gotterdammerung. RIGHT: *A Rhein maiden in* Rheingold.

operas: he created a new form of musical expression. "Continuous melody" follows the dramatic events on the stage. The orchestra—for which Wagner created new instruments, such as the Wagner tuba—expresses powerful emotions, and musically explains the psychology of his characters. You may have heard of Wagner's *leitmotive*—recurrent themes that express moods and ideas and identify the characters in the plot. These *leitmotive* are not mechanically put together like the bricks of a house. They are musical ideas that build the musical and dramatic structure. Some—like the ride of the galloping Walkyries, the sound of the waves of the Rhine—have descriptive character; others provide wonderful musical moods. Of Wagner's late masterpieces *Tristan and Isolde* is perhaps the greatest love poem set to music, with an expressive harmonic language of incredible power. The *Meistersinger* is remarkable for both humor and lyricism, for its rich polyphony and marvelous libretto; it would make a fine play even without music. Wagner, as I've said, wrote all his texts himself. You couldn't think of two

more different works than the death-love mood in *Tristan* or the down-to-earth fun in *Meistersinger*. Wagner's greatest achievement is his monumental *Ring*, meant to be given on four evenings during one week; all together some twenty-two hours of drama, action, symphony, excitement, with giants and gods, dragons and Rhine maidens, fantastic scenic effects (in *Götterdämmerung*, Walhalla, the castle of the gods, burns down in the end and is covered by the greenish waters of the Rhine) and musical climaxes unsurpassed in the history of music. Finally *Parsifal*, the most mature expression of the master's genius which, I feel, is a sort of nondenominational religious service—but very hard to understand, even for experienced Wagnerians.

You will hear Wagner's works—he is one of the most performed composers in the opera house—and if you will try to accept all the elements of his total theater you will be rewarded by some of the greatest excitement of the musical stage, despite the inevitable stretches of boredom. Believe me, it's worth trying.

LEFT: Lohengrin. BELOW: Tannhäuser.

111

EVERYBODY LOVES VERDI

A theater poster announcing the first performance of Verdi's Otello, *February 5, 1887.*

By one of Nature's inexplicable miracles, five months after the birth of Richard Wagner, a little peasant boy was born who became the other great dominating genius of our operatic stage. Giuseppe Verdi was often depicted as Wagner's great adversary—which is nonsense. Verdi was often haunted by Wagner and immensely impressed by the German master but he went his own way, and though both succeeded in the ultimate aim of the musical stage—to express humans and human emotions through drama and music—the great Italian genius is totally different from Wagner whom he outlived by eighteen years. Verdi was born in October 1813, in the sleepy village of Roncole, died in Milan at the age of ninety-one, and almost to the end of his life he gave us exciting opera. His youth falls into a heroic epoch of his Italian homeland. After the Napoleonic wars northern Italy was ruled by Austria, and there was a surge of patriotism and strife for independence. Great Italian writers such as Alessandro Manzoni and Silvio Pellico spoke up for Italy's liberty but no one said it better than Verdi did in an early opera, *Nabucco* (1842), in which he used the Biblical story of the oppressed Israelites after their defeat by Nebuchadnezzar, King of Babylon, to inflame the patriotism of his Italian countrymen. The magnificent chorus "Va Pensiero" ("Fly, O Thought") became the unofficial hymn of the Italians. At the age of thirty Verdi had become a popular hero in his homeland. Years later the sign VIVA VERDI, hastily painted on buildings in Milan, also stood for "Long Live Victor Emanuel Re d'Italia" and hailed the patriot musician and the future king of Italy.

Verdi continued to write operas: *Ernani* (1844), *I Masnadieri* (1847, after Schiller's *Robbers*) and *Luisa Miller* (1849), and retired to his lovely country estate St. Agata, raising livestock and hunting, reading Shakespeare, and composing. Work helped him to overcome the unhappiness after the loss of his beloved wife and two children. Within two years, 1851–1853 he composed *Rigoletto, Il Trovatore,* and *La Traviata,* three of the most universally loved

Giuseppe Verdi (1813–1901) brought melodic, rhythmic and dramatic genius to grand opera.

113

works of the operatic stage. All show the genius of Verdi whose wonderful feeling for melody and rhythm overcame the handicap of bad libretti. (To this day no one can really explain the improbable, melodramatic happenings in *Il Trovatore*, a story of passion and jealousy, and of brothers who fight because they don't know their blood relationship!) In the composer's earlier works the orchestral accompaniment is sometimes rather simple, in the manner of Donizetti. Suddenly there is a flash of genius, a wonderful melody, such as *"La Donna e Mobile"* ("Woman is Fickle") in *Rigoletto*, or *"Di quella pira"* ("Tremble, ye tyrants") in *Trovatore* which ends with a dramatic, immensely effective climax that never fails to rouse the audience if it's sung by a great tenor.

Verdi's melodies were so popular that they were often sung and whistled by people everywhere the day after the first performance. He expresses the Italian love of song and melody, tears and laughter, joy and sadness. If you love Italy—and most people do—you will love Verdi who translated the soul of Italy into music. By the time he wrote *Un Ballo in Maschera (A Masked Ball*, 1859), *La Forza del Destino (The Force of Destiny*, 1862), and *Don Carlo* (1867) after the drama of the same title by Friedrich Schiller, Verdi's style showed many of Wagner's characteristics; the continuous melody, the sense of musical drama, the feeling for great climaxes. But Verdi never tried to overwhelm his listeners as Wagner did. Verdi tried to immerse his listeners in music which expresses all feelings, and is easily understood by everybody. He also proved that a great composer can express emotion more deeply than the dramatist who uses only words.

In 1869 Verdi was commissioned to write an opera for the opening of the Suez Canal. He created *Aïda*, his most popular work, in the style of the "grand opera," but Verdi really produced a masterpiece of *great* opera. There are mass scenes and ballets and pomp—but there is also human passion and there are real people, involved in eternal problems: love and jealousy, treason and death. It is the story of

the Egyptian military commander Radames, who falls in love with Aïda, the beautiful Ethiopian slave. He betrays Egypt's strategy to Aïda who happens to be the daughter of the Ethiopian king Amonasro. It is a great tragedy that ends with the death of the two lovers.

Aïda has universal appeal and a certain Signor Bertani from Reggio, near Verdi's birthplace, is now remembered in the annals of opera because he did not like it. In a letter to Verdi he wrote that he had heard *Aïda* twice in nearby Parma, that "the opera contained nothing exciting," and asked the composer for a refund. Verdi instructed his publisher to pay back Bertani's money "provided he will sign a statement that he won't hear any more of Verdi's operas."

In 1874 Verdi composed his beautiful *Requiem Mass*, after the death of the admired Manzoni—a very exciting mass that is often performed on the concert stage. Then for thirteen years Verdi remained silent. He lived quietly and happily in St. Agata with his second wife, the singer Giuseppina Strepponi, looking after his grain fields and olives. But in 1887, at the age of seventy-three, he surprised the world with *Otello*, a work of genius from the opening "storm" scene to the tragic end of Othello. It is a perfect opera, the masterpiece of a wise old man with a young heart. *"E finito!"* ("It's finished!") Verdi wrote afterwards to his dramatist Arrigo Boïto (himself a composer and author of the exciting opera *Mefistofele*).

But it wasn't finished yet. In his eightieth year, Verdi began to write the most difficult thing of all, a comic opera. In 1892 *Falstaff* was completed, again with a libretto by Boïto based on Shakespeare's play. I think Shakespeare wouldn't mind it if he could hear Verdi's *Falstaff*, the perfect musical comedy, charming and witty and wise. With Mozart's *Figaro*, Wagner's *Meistersinger*, and Strauss' *Rosenkavalier*, *Falstaff* belongs to our treasury of the finest musical humor. The first act of *Falstaff* is probably Verdi's greatest music.

The kindly old man with the little butterfly tie is now the most universally beloved of all operatic composers.

TOP, LEFT: *Giuseppina Strepponi, Verdi's second wife.*
TOP, RIGHT: *A scene from* Falstaff.

ABOVE: *A scene from the most popular of Verdi's operas,* Aïda. Aïda *has everything—spectacle, pageantry, pomp, scenes of love, jealousy and revenge and, above all, a musical score of enduring beauty.*

115

OPERA IN PARIS

GEORGES BIZET (1838–1875) is not in the same league with his two contemporaries, Verdi and Wagner, but he wrote an opera that probably will be performed forever. *Carmen* has a perfect story, with beautiful melodies, great arias, exciting choruses, great force, and with its style of *verismo* (dramatic truth) Bizet created a whole school in opera. It is a wonderful drama, full of southern temperament—the action takes place in Spain—and opera lovers all over the world always admire it. Today *Carmen* is acknowledged as one of the few "perfect" operas (there are really only half a dozen of them, as we have seen). But *Carmen* was a failure when it was first performed in Paris in 1875, and Bizet, suffering from a heart ailment, died a broken man a few months later at the age of thirty-seven. Now he is considered a far greater composer than his compatriots Charles Gounod (1818–1893), who is best known for his *Faust;* or Jules Massenet (1842–1912), whose *Manon* is a work of tender charm and elegant style; or Camille Saint-Saëns (1835–1921), whose *Samson et Dalila* is a great improvement over the French "grand opera"; or Ambroise Thomas (1811–1896), who wrote *Mignon,* a work popular in France.

A Belgian composer of much greater importance is César Franck (1822–1890). He began as an organist and later wrote beautiful oratorios, chamber music, symphonic poems, and the celebrated D-minor symphony. Franck was a master of polyphony and sometimes he reached moments of great beauty and spiritual power. Many people think of Franck in connection with his contemporary, the Austrian composer Anton Bruckner. They were different in their background and their methods but both were deeply religious men who always sing the praise of God.

At the same time there was in France a man whose work is now fully recognized. Jacques Offenbach (1819-1880), the son of the cantor of the Cologne synagogue, came to Paris as a young man and became the popular composer of witty, ironic, graceful French operettas that made fun of pompous stuffed shirts and men in

The Paris Opera House, in a photograph taken in 1900.

116

power. The best known are *Orpheus in Hades*, *Parisian Life*, *Fair Helen*. His librettists, Meilhac and Halévy, who had written the excellent book of *Carmen*, wrote entertaining libretti for Offenbach. His masterpiece is a serious work, *Tales of Hoffmann*, which shows his special gift for tragedy. It is a fascinating opera with many hidden meanings, as fantastic as the man after whom it is called—E. T. A. Hoffmann, the strange romanticist, who wrote stark horror stories.

TOP LEFT: *Jacques Offenbach (1819–1880).* BOTTOM LEFT: *Charles Gounod (1818–1893).* ABOVE: *A scene from Bizet's* verismo *opera* Carmen, *the most frequently performed opera in the repertoire.* BELOW: *Mephistopheles bargains with Faust for his soul in this scene from Gounod's well-known opera.*

BRAHMS, BRUCKNER, MAHLER

August Rodin's bust of Gustav Mahler (1860–1911).

JOHANNES BRAHMS was born in Hamburg in 1833, came to Vienna when he was thirty, and died there in 1897. He was a real romanticist; there was melancholy in his soul and always a longing in his life. Beethoven was his idol and he loved the old masters of polyphony. His four symphonies, written between 1876 and 1885, are performed everywhere; powerful, melodic, melancholy, with deep feeling. Some of Brahms' movements have the exuberance of a fast Haydn movement, others the sadness of Beethoven or the melodic wealth of Schubert, but they are always Brahms. His two piano concertos, the difficult and very beautiful violin concerto, the magnificent double concerto for violin, cello and orchestra, his chamber music, and his *German Requiem* are really masterpieces. People sometimes think he is "heavy" and his music is often, especially in Germany, performed with a pedantic seriousness which ruins its poetic content. But when you hear his *lieder,* when you think of his immortal *Wiegenlied (Lullaby),* his poetic piano music full of charm and elegance, his beautiful variations on a theme by Haydn, you will realize that Brahms is an important composer close to our hearts because he understands our thoughts and our feelings. He was a generous man who had kind words for other composers. When he heard the beautiful *Blue Danube* waltz by Johann Strauss, Vienna's "waltz king," and was asked for an autograph by Strauss' wife, Brahms wrote the first measures of the waltz and underneath, "Unfortunately not by—Johannes Brahms." But when he was in a bad mood, he would insult everybody in his company. One night he got up from his table at the beer-house where he sat with his friends, and said, "If anyone is here whom I did *not* insult, I apologize." Then he walked out.

Hans von Bülow called Bach, Beethoven, and Brahms "the three great B's." Today there is a fourth great B—Anton Bruckner, who is taking on the stature of a giant, still widely misunderstood, but a master of tremendous force. Bruckner (1824–1896), the son of a poor schoolmaster musician from Ansfelden in Aus-

118

tria, began as a choirboy in the St. Florian monastery, where he later worked as organist, and where he is buried. His contemporaries didn't understand his symphonies which are long, powerful, and monumental. Today many of us think of him as a modern Beethoven. The slow movements and the scherzi reflect Beethoven's influence. But Bruckner can only be understood as a devout Catholic; he wanted to create for the greater glory of God; and he is happiest when he is in heaven, making music with the angels, and only reluctantly does he come back to earth. It is not easy to penetrate his nine symphonies, which are like giant cathedrals—not unlike Bach's choral works—filled with themes that are often repeated. But the more you listen to Bruckner, the more you are impressed; he may, like Schubert, suffer from "divine length," but he touches your heart. His critics say that he is lacking in "form," but he certainly has conviction and power. He wrote great masses too, and his use of brass instruments and tremolos is impressive! He is probably the man of the future; every year more people are caught by the magnificence of Bruckner's symphonic hymns.

Gustav Mahler (1860–1911) is often compared to Bruckner. It is true that both were Austrian, that both composed powerful symphonies and that both were deeply religious men but otherwise they have little in common. While Bruckner performs in heaven, letting the angels play their horns, Mahler stays on earth, suffering with his fellow men.

Mahler, one of the best conductors of all time and an artist of impeccable style who recreated the world of Mozart to its glory, is a master of orchestration—the art of writing for orchestra. It was only toward the end of the nineteenth century, when the size of orchestras increased, that composers began to annotate their scores more carefully. Haydn in Eisenstadt or Beethoven in Vienna would *tell* their musicians how the music should be played. It was Wagner who, wanting new colors from his orchestra, began to write down the effect he desired. And Gustav Mahler's scores have the most exact

markings of all. Mahler knew, for instance, that the flute sounds weaker in certain positions and stronger in others. Sometimes he wrote *piano* for the flute knowing it would sound like *mezzoforte*. If every player plays his part in a Mahler symphony exactly as it is written, he cannot go wrong. Mahler's most famous work is his sorrowful *Lied von der Erde* (*Song of the Earth*), where he shows himself as a great lyricist; and he wrote some fine and deeply felt songs. Mahler's influence, like Bruckner's, is steadily growing. He is especially popular in the United States where his great pupil Bruno Walter did much to introduce audiences to the often dark and difficult world of this great musician.

Anton Bruckner (1824–1896).

119

RICHARD STRAUSS & PUCCINI

AUSTERITY certainly was not in the vocabulary of Richard Strauss, born in Munich in 1864 (and no relation to the Viennese-waltz Strauss family). He comes from a musical family and studied piano, violin, harmony and composition. You have noticed that some composers' fame increases after their death while others are almost forgotten. The fame of Strauss seems to have decreased. There is a widespread tendency among high-brow critics now to underrate Richard Strauss in spite of the fact that his music is still widely played. The critics say disparagingly that he was a virtuoso of "program music" and that he composed without effort. But after you've heard some of his "tone poems" such as *Till Eulenspiegel's Merry Pranks*, or *Don Quixote*, or *Death and Transfiguration*, you will perhaps realize that it is easy and dangerous to call this music "program music," as though you would have to read the program to know what it is all about. I believe that such virtuosity as Strauss had is already an art; and could he help it that he was extremely gifted? True, he started out under the influence of Mendelssohn and Brahms, later fought against the influence of Wagner, and finally attained his aim to write in the lucid style of Mozart, who was his great ideal. But in his virtuoso hand every score became truly personal —with magnificent harmony, beautiful melody, and exciting (almost Wagnerian) climaxes.

Strauss started out writing for the symphony orchestra, but his sense of drama and his love for the stage took him to the opera house. (He was also an acclaimed conductor in his time, especially good in Mozart and Wagner.) *Salome*, his first important work, caused such a scandal in Vienna that Emperor Franz Joseph I forbade it to be performed at the Court Opera. It was too shocking to see a young girl drop her seven veils while dancing for her stepfather, and Strauss' music was even more shocking. His next work, a one-act "horror-show" called *Elektra* (1909), assured him a safe place on the list of the immortal composers. The old Sophocles drama retold by the Viennese poet Hugo von Hofmannsthal—who became the librettist of Strauss' finest work—begins and ends with the terrifying "Agamemnon" motif, and in between there are 100 minutes of unrelenting horror and shock. But there is also tender beauty and unmistakable genius. His most popular opera is *Der Rosenkavalier;* it has a wonderful libretto by Hofmannsthal, fine music, great waltz melodies and beautiful harmonies. The experts, however, prefer *Ariadne auf Naxos*—where Strauss once more departs into his beloved world of Greek mythology—and his monumental work *Die Frau ohne Schatten* (*The Woman without a Shadow,* 1919). Although Hofmannsthal's libretto for this opera is obscure and full of symbolism (it is the story of a woman who has no children and wants to buy the "shadow" of another woman who can have children), Strauss' music is magnificent—some of the finest he ever wrote. The Metropolitan Opera in New York paid homage to Strauss and the work by giving this opera at its new house at Lincoln Center during the initial season. Strauss died at the age of eighty-seven in 1949. Five years earlier he had completed his brilliant short opera *Capriccio,* joining the ranks of great octogenarian composers.

I have now mentioned the major composers of our operatic stage—Mozart, Verdi, Wagner, Strauss. There remains Giacomo Puccini (1858–1924), as popular as ever, snubbed by the highbrows, and loved by all people who love music and melody. Puccini knew the secret of writing beautiful operas; he could make people laugh or cry. His works reveal melodic invention, strange harmonies, beautiful orchestration. Like his countryman Verdi, he wrote wonderful arias, and performed wonders with chords and intervals. He is dearly loved by tenors, prima donnas, and the managers of all opera houses who know that a performance of *La Bohème* or *Madame Butterfly* will always sell out. Millions of people cannot be wrong. There is tender beauty in *La Bohème,* exciting passion in *Tosca,* and everything from moving arias to powerful choruses in *Turandot,* perhaps Puccini's masterpiece. He died in 1924, before he could finish the score. It was later completed by the composer Franco Alfano following Puccini's sketches and notes. During the premiere of *Turandot* at Milan's La Scala, Arturo Toscanini, the great friend of Puccini, stopped the orchestra in the third act, turned to the audience, and said with tears in his eyes, "Here the Maestro died." Then he continued the performance.

No other operatic composer of his time reached Puccini's popularity. Pietro Mascagni was successful with *Cavalleria Rusticana,* which is often given on the same bill with another short work, Leoncavallo's *Pagliacci.* There is much violent action, passion, and murder in these operas, and the music has naturalistic effects. This is the school of *verismo* (veracity). Other works belonging in this group are d'Albert's *Tiefland,* Rabaud's *Marouf,* and Umberto Giordano's *Andrea Chénier.* He comes closest to Puccini.

OPPOSITE: *Giacomo Puccini (1858–1924). His operas brought the* verismo *style to its greatest peak.*

BELOW: *Richard Strauss (1864–1949) carried program music to a high art in his popular tone poems.*

PART V
NATIONAL MUSIC

THE IMPRESSIONISTS

Claude Debussy (1862–1918) was the leader of the impressionists.

*W*E have now reached the contemporary period. It is not yet "twelve-tone music" but it is new music based on new ideas. The greatest musical invention of the period that followed Richard Wagner is impressionism. In the art of painting, the impressionist artist treats a subject as though he were seeing it for a fleeting moment—he has an "impression" which he puts on the canvas. In literature and in music, impressionism creates similar results. The music is full of atmospheric effects: in Debussy's *La Mer* you may close your eyes and will hear the waves of the sea. It is poetry that has been turned into music. A landscape, a mood, a feeling are expressed by tone colors. The musical impressionists use tones and dynamic nuances exactly as Renoir and Monet use colors and lights. There are fleeting moments that excite the ear—and are gone. Instead of the classicist "form" there is "atmosphere." The trombones are muted, the woodwinds play in the lower registers, the drums are muffled, and the violins play delicate themes. The orchestration is shimmering, making you think of the landscape poetry of the French impressionist painters.

It is a French movement, in music as well as in painting. Claude Debussy, born in Saint-German-en-Laye in 1862, had been under the influence of Massenet and Wagner. Then he began to develop the harmonic system that he brought to such perfection. Debussy's music is already extremely modern in our sense of the word: it is oversensitive and restless, poetically inspired, and always intriguing. It is very beautiful music; and Debussy was the only real inventor in music at the turn of our century. His masterpiece is *Pelléas et Mélisande*, based on a famous book by the Belgian poet Maeterlinck. It is called an opera, but it is unlike any other piece performed in the theater. It is almost like a dream come true; it is sheer poetry. The singing is often close to spoken declamation, while the orchestra contributes the musical impressions. Other composers have done impressionistic descriptions, from Beethoven to Wagner, but in Debussy's work the musical

Edgar Degas, The Musicians of the Orchestra. *The impressionists exploited to the full the tone colors of the orchestra.*

impressions are part of the dramatic tension. The music of *Pelléas* often sounds as if it had been done by a composer painting with music; it is diffused, and the outlines are often blurred. But it would be wrong to make this music sound as if it were performed behind a curtain. Some artists, even famous ones, perform Debussy's music as if it had been written in a thick fog. Debussy himself liked to have his music played with transparent clarity so that the contours were visible. Only a bad artist escapes into the fog of ambiguity. Debussy's musical impressions are as clear as the impressions painted by Manet or Renoir. He is a very French composer, like his great predecessors Couperin and Rameau. His *L'Après-Midi d'un Faune* (*The Afternoon of a Faun*) will fascinate you with new sounds, new colors. Debussy wrote *Images and Nocturnes* for orchestra, and in his latest works *Le Martyre de Saint Sébastien* (*The Martyrdom of St. Sebastian*) and *Jeux* he already foreshadows the later trends of Webern and other moderns.

Debussy's "aesthetic revolution" was apparent in 1893, when the Ysaÿe Quartet performed his magnificent string quartet. It has been compared to Ravel's string quartet but each is a masterpiece in its own way. Debussy's piano music shows his new inventions, his new technique. All composers after Debussy were influenced by him—though not all admit it. He was bitterly criticized and had no wide public but his admirers made up for his lack of popular appeal by their enthusiasm.

Maurice Ravel (1875–1937) was long believed to be an "imitator" of Debussy perhaps because there are impressionistic tone colors in his music. Today Ravel is recognized as a gifted composer who developed his own brilliant style and cannot be compared with anyone. Ravel writes virtuoso music for virtuoso performers, and in our time, which values technical perfection, he is much admired. He was much more than a technician; he was a fine musician who created superb orchestral effects. His *Daphnis et Chloé* suite is a dazzling virtuoso composition which needs a first-rate orchestra under a first-rate conductor. When the late Paul Wittgenstein—a celebrated Austrian pianist who lost his right arm in World War I—asked Ravel to write something for him, Ravel composed his famous *Concerto for the Left Hand*. When you hear a recording it's hard to believe that the pianist in this exciting work with strong jazz rhythms and terrific bravura runs, performs only with the left hand. Such virtuosity is apparent in all of Ravel's work—his songs, his piano pieces, his brilliant string quartet, his stage works *L'Heure espagnole* and *L'Enfant et les Sortilèges*. His best-known orchestra works are *La Valse*,

ABOVE: *Maurice Ravel (1875–1937) carried on and enriched the impressionistic traditions of Debussy.* RIGHT: *A page from Ravel's* Chansons Madecasses, *written in 1925–26.*

Ravel's brilliant apotheosis of a waltz theme, and his *Boléro*, a celebrated tour de force that made him world-famous. Ravel takes a simple Spanish dance theme which is played by different instruments and sections of the orchestra and eventually ends in a magnificent *fortissimo* climax, played by the entire orchestra. It never fails to impress the audience, and is dearly beloved both by orchestra musicians and conductors.

Impressionism was the most important musical school in France in the early years of our century, and other musicians were often classified in their relationship to impressionism. It is always dangerous to classify an artist; each creative man is basically himself. Vincent d'Indy (1851–1931) was called a "reactionary" by the followers of Debussy and a "revolutionary" by the conservatives. Actually he was a composer with great lyrical feeling, love of his native land, and a fine craftsman. Gabriel Fauré (1845–1924) is very much admired in France but little understood elsewhere. He writes subtle, transparent music—the French call his style *souplesse*, subtlety—but he often makes one think of Schumann and Franck. His songs are elegant and exquiste, truly French. Paul Dukas (1865–1935) has been called "a French Richard Strauss" perhaps because he handled his orches-

tra with great skill. His symphonic poem *The Sorcerer's Apprentice*, a brilliant orchestral scherzo, reminds one of Strauss' orchestral work *Till Eulenspiegel*. Dukas was a perfectionist who destroyed, unfortunately, every score that didn't seem perfect to him. He almost destroyed *La Péri* which is now considered a masterpiece of contemporary ballet. Another Frenchman, Florent Schmitt (1870–1959) was a classmate of Ravel when both studied composition with Fauré. Schmitt's craftsmanship is also very delicate but he is little performed outside of France today.

Erik Satie (1866–1925) is still something of a mystery. His first piano pieces, published in 1886, show audacious harmonies, and many claimed that he paved the way for Debussy, but today Debussy's originality is no longer questioned. Later Satie wrote brief pieces with humorous or satirical connotations reacting against the "mist" of the impressionists or the "sublimity" of Wagner and Franck. Albert Roussel (1869–1937) experimented with different styles, and in his earlier years was thought to be an impressionist. But in his last twenty years he developed his own style which has been adopted by various composers—very striking rhythms, flowing melodies in the slow movements, exotic harmonies, and a gift for lyricism.

ABOVE: *Critics—and satirists—compared Gabriel Fauré's way of composing to a woman doing a piece of embroidery—so meticulous was his craftsmanship.* LEFT: *Debussy was also a fine craftsman, as can be seen in the care with which he prepared his manuscripts. Here is a page from his opera* Pelléas et Mélisande.

THE RUSSIANS & STRAVINSKY

Peter Illyitch Tchaikovsky (1840–1893) was Russia's first "professional" composer. His works still make up a large part of the concert repertoire today.

*I*N Russia, "national" music began only in the nineteenth century when Russian composers began to exploit Russian folklore. Michael Ivanovich Glinka (1804–1857) studied in Germany. But after the success of his opera *Life for the Tsar*, given in Russia in 1836, many Russian musicians realized that at last they now had their own national music, as other nations had. Other composers of that era were Alexander Dargomirsky, hardly known outside Russia, and Anton Rubinstein, a brilliant pianist and an imitator of Mendelssohn and Schumann. Then came Mili Balakirev (1837–1910), a self-taught composer with strong opinions—he said that Bach was "too abstract" and Mozart "too frivolous"—who admired Glinka and wrote in the new Russian style. He had four remarkable disciples who were amateurs: Cesar Cui, engineering professor who wrote many songs and orchestra pieces; Alexander Borodin, professor of chemistry, who played four instruments and "wrote one fugue every day," is best known for his opera *Prince Igor;* and two professional officers, Modeste Mussorgsky (1839–1881), who served in the army, and Nicholas Rimsky-Korsakov (1844–1881), a navy man.

Of this "Group of Five," Mussorgsky was the most gifted. He discovered the soul of Russia in his music; you will hear his masterpiece *Boris Godunov,* the greatest musical drama of Eastern Europe, whose protagonist is not the Czar, but the people of Russia, interpreted by powerful choruses. Mussorgsky showed the Russian people to the West as Tolstoy and Dostoyevsky did in their great novels. He has been called the founder of musical realism, but such terms are narrow and didactic. *Boris* is a great masterpiece, primitive and shocking and full of power. One finds this power also in *Khovanchina* and in his symphonic poem *Night on the Bare Mountain* which was orchestrated from his sketches by his friend Rimsky-Korsakov (Ravel orchestrated Mussorgsky's powerful piano piece *Pictures at an Exhibition*). And it was Rimsky-Korsakov who set out to correct what he thought were mistakes in Mussorgsky's harmonies in *Boris*. In recent times

126

he has been bitterly criticized for "doctoring" the work of his friend, and the original, unchanged *Boris* of Mussorgsky is again performed. Actually Rimsky-Korsakov had the best intention. "If it is felt that the original is better than my version, *Boris* can be given in the original form . . . " he wrote. He composed fifteen operas, the most popular being *Sadko* and *Le Coq d'Or*.

The best known Russian composer, and one of the most popular names in today's concert halls and opera houses, is Peter Ilyitch Tchaikovsky (1840–1893), Russia's first "professional" composer. He is also an "international" composer, but still thoroughly Russian. Many critics have called him a "sentimentalist," and it is true that his symphonies contain banalities and stretches of emptiness. But at his best he writes beautiful, elegant, and powerful Russian music, and it is admitted that his *Pathétique Symphony* is the most effective symphony ever composed, equally beloved by conductors and their audiences. Unfortunately his works have become so popular that they are imitated to death. Among his operas *Eugen Onegin* and *Pique Dame* are masterpieces, and so are the ballets *Swan Lake*, *Nutcracker* and *The Sleeping Princess*, his overtures "*1812*" and *Romeo and Juliet*, his chamber music works, his songs, and his effective violin concerto. It is certainly an exaggeration to call Tchaikovsky "the Russian Beethoven." There was only one Beethoven. But Tchaikovsky is a great and popular musician. His music is understood and loved by millions of people.

There are other gifted composers in Russia—Glazunov, Arensky, Liadow, Rachmaninov (whose concertos and symphonies are now widely performed), but the immortal Russian name in music is Igor Stravinsky. Born at Oranienbaum in 1882, he took his first music lesson with Rimsky-Korsakov. In his thirties Stravinsky wrote several ballets that made him world-famous: the *Firebird*, *Petroushka*, *Rites of Spring*, *Nightingale*. They are astonishing works, even today. Stravinsky gave up his early infatuation with impressionism and created his own style, a

Nicholas Rimsky-Korsakov (1844–1881) drew heavily on Russian history and folklore for the inspiration for his compositions.

very personal harmonic language, and very strong rhythms. On May 29, 1913, when *Rites of Spring* was first performed in Paris, it created one of the famous scandals in the annals of music. The audience assumed that a monstrous joke was being perpetrated, and both Stravinsky and his conductor, Pierre Monteux, had to escape through a window from the furious listeners. Some people even feel that way now when they hear the music, in which Stravinsky tries to give the idea of primeval life emerging from chaos. Fifty years after its premiere *Rites of Spring* still is one terrific shock effect. For many years thereafter, modern composers were under the influence of Stravinsky's asymmetric rhythms and his percussion passages.

Since then Stravinsky has tried new ways of expression in *The Soldier's Tale, Oedipus Rex, The Rake's Progress*. After a period when he created in the neoclassic style, going back to Bach and the early classics of Vienna, he has employed the jovial technique of Webern and Schoenberg. He has already left his imprint on music, and posterity will perhaps rank him with the great innovators such as Monteverdi, Wagner, or Debussy. He is not a "Russian" composer, did not return to the Soviet Union, and now lives in the United States; but the Russians honored him greatly when he went back there on a short visit in 1962.

The greatest Russian composer of our era was Serge Prokofiev (1891–1953) who was a master of machine-like rhythm and great melodic invention. Sometimes the rhythm in Prokofiev's music makes you think of the noise in a factory, mechanical and repetitious, but he can also be lyrical, as in his *Classical Symphony*, and his works *Lieutenant Kije* and *Peter and the Wolf* show real genius. *Peter and the Wolf* is perhaps the most charming piece of music ever written especially for young people.

Among contemporary Russian composers, Dimitri Shostakovitch, born in 1906, is the most gifted. When he entered the Leningrad Conservatory at the age of thirteen, he showed such promise that Glazunov gave him a scholarship out of his own pocket for the period of his

studies. In his first symphonies, his operas *The Nose* and *Lady Macbeth of Mzensk* he developed great originality. But in contemporary Russia a composer cannot create as he feels; he must write according to the "Party line." Shostakovitch was in trouble several times for "deviationist" tendencies. It is uncertain how he would write if he lived outside the Soviet Union. But since he lives there, he must conform to the ideas of the political commissars who know nothing about music.

128

OPPOSITE, TOP: *Igor Stravinsky (1882–) conducting at a recording session.* OPPOSITE, BOTTOM: *A portrait of Serge Prokofiev (1891–1953) by the Russian artist Natalia Gontcharova.* ABOVE: *A costume design by Pablo Picasso for the Stravinsky suite* Pulcinella.

SMETANA, DVOŘÁK, JANÁČEK

AMONG other Slavonic nations the inhabitants of Moravia and Bohemia (today parts of Czechoslovakia) are the most music-minded. For centuries "Bohemian musicians" were known all over Europe. Music is the most vibrant expression of the Bohemian and Moravian countryside. In his great symphonic poem *My Fatherland*, Bedřich Smetana (1824–1884), the most famous Bohemian composer, has written a magnificent musical portrait of his beloved homeland; you probably have heard the lovely second part, called *Moldau*, the story of a mighty river. In the villages of the countryside people were always dancing and singing. It is no accident that Mozart was better understood in Prague than in his Vienna, that his *Don Giovanni* was first performed at the old National Theater in Prague, for centuries the meeting place of famous musicians. Many composers working at the time of Haydn, Mozart, and Beethoven came from Bohemia and Moravia.

The music of Smetana is the musical expression of his homeland. In his masterpiece *The Bartered Bride*, which is Czechoslovakia's "national" opera, he evokes the spirit of the people, the melodies hovering about the meadows and forests, the dance rhythms, the nostalgia, and the happiness. It is one of the few genuinely comic operas. In addition to his orchestra music, Smetana also wrote chamber music. His famous string quartet *From My Life* is Smetana's musical autobiography. It begins happily and ends in tragedy. Like Beethoven, Smetana became totally deaf at the end of his life.

Antonin Dvořák (1841–1904) is loved for his symphonies and *Slavonic Dances*, and for his chamber music. In all his work he is completely a product of his homeland, although he sometimes seems to have been under the influence of Wagner and Brahms. He spent a few years in the United States and created there his *New World Symphony* (1893), one of the most often performed and recorded works of the repertory, in which he uses Indian rhythms and evokes the nostalgia of the émigré in his moving "Going home" theme. The same haunting music is in his "American" string quartet, dear to the

A design for Smetana's The Bartered Bride.

Bedrich Smetana (1824–1884).

hearts of all string players.

But probably the greatest Czech musician would be Leoš Janáček (1854–1928) from Moravia, one of the genuine innovators and inventors, who created a totally new, immensely modern conception of harmony and counterpoint. His masterpiece, the opera *Jenufa*, is now being discovered everywhere, and so is his symphonic music, especially his beautiful *Sinfonietta*. Janáček is one of the few genuine modern Czech composers. None of those who came later— Vitězlav Novák, Alois Hába, Bohuslav Martinu —is up to his greatness.

LEFT: *Leoš Janáček (1854–1928).* ABOVE: *Antonin Dvořák (1841–1904). With Smetana and Janáček, Dvořák's music was inspired by his love of his country.*

MUSIC IN MANY COUNTRIES

AMONG the English composers of the era we must remember Sir Arthur Sullivan (1842–1900) who wrote fine choral and orchestral works and with Sir William Gilbert (1836–1911) created comic operas that made their names a household word in the English speaking world. You may have enjoyed *The Mikado*. Sir Edward Elgar (1857–1934), a fine classicist, is very much beloved in England. Elsewhere it is felt that his music reflects Wagner and Brahms and Liszt and Strauss—but not enough of Elgar. The gifted Benjamin Britten (1913–   ) has made significant contributions to English opera. Two American composers, Edward MacDowell (1861–1908) and Horatio William Parker (1863–1919) showed good craftsmanship and solid taste in their works.

The national music of the Scandinavian countries is also dominated by a rich folklore and old traditions. Poetry and song always flourished in these countries, but as in Russia an original national music developed rather late. Denmark's best composer, Niels Gade (1817–1890) wrote in the spirit of Mendelssohn and Schumann. Norway's musical hero is Edvard Grieg (1843–1907) whom you know from his piano concerto, the *Norwegian Dances*, the *Peer Gynt Suite*. His music has poetic charm, clear rhythms and lyrical invention. Perhaps the most admired composer in this part of the world was Jan Sibelius (1865–1957), Finland's contribution to the world of music. His dark, somber symphonic poems (*Finlandia*, *The Swan of Tuonela*) evoke the impressive atmosphere of his homeland, with its lakes and forests and dark skies. He is greatly admired and much performed in the Anglo-Saxon countries, where his seven symphonies are popular, but elsewhere people feel that he is not always original and often monotonous in his lonely grandeur.

In Poland, Stanislav Moniuszko's opera *Halka* is the "national" opera, but it has never succeeded elsewhere. A more interesting composer is Karl Szymanowski (1882–1937) who started out under the influence of Strauss and Debussy but evoked his own national style. His piano music, his Second Violin Concerto, his symphonies are fine music.

Rumania's best known musician is Georges Enesco (1881–1955), a famous violinist who became a first -rate composer. In his symphonies and sonatas there are many traces of Rumanian folklore. Far more brilliant is the musical life in neighboring Hungary. As in all countries long oppressed by a foreign regime, the music is dominated by folklore, intensely national—in this case the haunting songs of the countryside and the exciting rhythms and harmonies of the Hungarian gypsies. In Hungary, some exciting folkloristic music was written by Ernö Dohnányi (1877–1960), and by Zoltán Kodály (born in 1882), today admired as Hungary's great old man of music. His masterpiece *Psalmus Hungaricus* shows the influence of Debussy, but remains strongly Hungarian. Like Debussy, Kodály is a master orchestrator.

The greatest Hungarian composer, and one of the greatest anywhere, is Béla Bartók. He was born in 1881, and died in 1945 in New York—sick, destitute, and all but forgotten. He is no longer forgotten, and the fame of Bartók increases steadily. He began composing under the influence of Debussy, Stravinsky, and Schoenberg. But Bartók soon found his own style—full of the memories and the haunting melodies of the Hungarian countryside—always in a personal, modern way. His immensely difficult *Concerto for Orchestra* is now a celebrated tour de force for the world's best orchestras. His piano music, his violin concerto, the pantomime *The Miraculous Mandarin,* and his folk songs are performed everywhere. It is not easy to play or to understand his music, but when it is well performed it makes a lasting impression. He was no compromiser: he wrote as he felt. The greatness and depth of his six string quartets, with their moments of personal suffering, remind one of Beethoven's last quartets. The day may come when Bartók will be one of the great "B's" together with Bach and Beethoven.

Let us look briefly at the Latin countries. In Italy symphonic music was revived by Ottorino Respighi (1879–1937) with his colorful, impressionistic tone poems *The Pines of Rome* and *The Fountains of Rome.* Ildebrando Pizzetti goes back to ancient modes but uses a modern idiom, and is renowned as an operatic composer. Among the modern Italians are Gian-Francesco Malipiero, composer of symphonic and chamber music; and Luigi Dallapiccola who writes in the "twelve-tone" system which will be discussed soon.

The two major Spanish composers are Isaac Albéniz (1860–1909) and Manuel de Falla (1876–1946). They write in different styles, but both reflect their Spanish heritage and both are very gifted. Albéniz composes as Debussy might have composed if he'd been Spanish; his finest work is *Iberia.* De Falla too writes in a beautiful, expressive manner, with great perfection; he never wrote any mediocre music. His *Nights in the Gardens of Spain, La Vida breve,* his *Songs* ("imaginary folklore") give a fine musical picture of Spain. And in South America we must mention Carlos Chavez in Mexico (born in 1899) who borrows from Indian music, while in Brazil Heitor Villa-Lobos (1887–1959) has composed in a very personal style, combining old European music with Brazilian melodies.

PART VI
MODERN
MUSIC

SCHOENBERG,
BERG, WEBERN

The first page of Webern's Variations for Piano, op. 27.

You may have heard about a certain modern music which some people call "atonal." Webster defines "tonality" as the "principle of key in music," which means that a piece written in the key of C major is based on a fixed relationship of the tones of the scale. An atonal piece, then, would be one that does not depend on key. It was Schoenberg who first composed such music, although he objected to its being called atonal. He described it as "twelve-tone music." The twelve half-tones of the scale are arranged in a fixed sequence, called a row, and this row must be used completely before it can start over again. But to provide variety, it may be turned upside down and read backward, devices somewhat reminiscent of the "learned" tricks of medieval music or Bach. Such music has no "melody" in the old sense of music and is full of strange sounds and dissonances. But Schoenberg predicted that a time would come when people would find dissonances "quite natural," and would understand dissonant music. Young people understand this music much better than the older generation brought up on Bach, Haydn, Mozart, Beethoven.

Oddly enough, the modern school of music originated in Vienna, once the center of classical music. Arnold Schoenberg was born there in 1874. (He died in Los Angeles in 1951.) He began his career in the post-Wagnerian iodiom of Strauss and Mahler, and some of his early works have become almost popular, such as his *Gurre-Lieder* and the string sextet *Transfigured Night*. But more and more he felt that the musical language as it was used by Beethoven or Wagner or Mahler had reached the end of its possibilities. These composers and others, had expanded the range of tonality, sometimes to a point where one could no longer say a work was composed in a certain key. In his own compositions Schoenberg noticed this trend very strongly and at one point he drew the radical consequence of abandoning key altogether. The twelve half-tones of the scale became independent of each other, there was no longer any relationship to a central key. The principle of tonality that had ruled music for three hundred years, just as modality had ruled it before, gave way to a new system that many people quite logically called atonality, although to Schoenberg himself this word was an abomination. He used this new system—later called twelve-tone system, dodecaphonic, or serial music—almost continually from about 1924 onward. After World War II the system spread rapidly all over the world, even to Russia. But by then it was not so much Schoenberg, whose music always betrays its romantic origins and conventional structure, but rather his pupil Anton von Webern who became the dominant influence. Webern (1883–1945) sometimes wrote very short pieces that are almost mathematical problems. One piece uses nine instruments and lasts only nineteen seconds. They are clear and transparent, have no audible melody and no apparent meaning, but are built like tiny transistors. The music is always quiet, every instrument plays a different score which creates a great variety of tone color, so one doesn't hear a central tonality. The music is a kaleidoscope in which the musical colors change all the time. There is a short tremolo on the flute, followed by an isolated *pizzicato;* then there is a short pause, harmonics, another pause. And so on. To many of us the meaning of this music is not clear. It does not touch the heart, it merely intrigues the mind. Perhaps this is the music of the next generation. One cannot be sure yet.

Schoenberg's other influential pupil was Alban Berg, who was born in Vienna in 1885 and died there in 1935. His *Wozzeck* is probably the most successful modern opera. I admit, when I first heard it I heard mostly sounds. Today I hear melodies and harmonies expressing ideas, sensations, and emotions; everything is clear. No wonder that today *Wozzeck* is almost a "classic" among modern works. Berg's violin concerto, which introduces a theme from a Bach chorale, is often performed and understood.

Don't think that the atonal composers just wanted to create "sound effects." They follow rigid forms. *Wozzeck* consists of a number of strict musical forms—fugue, sonata, scherzo. But the success of *Wozzeck* is due to the libretto

(a famous play by Büchner) and to the fact that *Wozzeck* indeed does move the heart. It is the story of a poor, abused soldier whom life treats shabbily. We suffer with Wozzeck, we are moved by him. Music, even modern music, should do something to us—it should excite, move, please, depress us. It should never be boring.

The most recent music has gone far beyond the atonal composers, even Webern. Some of it makes as little sense to me as do certain modern paintings where I don't know which side is up and which is down. I have sat unhappily through evenings of modern music, hearing only disconnected noises, and wishing it were over. But younger people tell me they can hear certain things and get certain impressions. To many composers of today and their admirers Schoenberg is "old hat."

A sketch of Schoenberg's most famous pupil, Alban Berg, made in 1935, the year of his death.

MUSIC IN THE UNITED STATES

George Gershwin photographed in his most characteristic pose by Edward Steichen.

MUSICAL life in the United States has been infinitely enriched by several waves of immigration and two world wars that brought some of the world's great composers and finest performers to the United States. It has slowly become known in Europe, where almost all great Western music was written, that the great American symphony orchestras are now the best in the world. In the United States, many great musicians have achieved a fine synthesis of old tradition with new technique. Gustav Mahler, the great Austrian composer-conductor, and Arturo Toscanini, the greatest Italian conductor of our century who spent the last twenty years of his life in this country, have introduced the principle of uncompromising artistic truth. No longer would musicians dare take liberties with a score, make changes, perform their own version. The composer is the undisputed boss, and the music must be performed as the composer wrote it. Naturally we don't know how the music of Mozart sounded to him. Probably the slow tempi have become slower in the past hundred years and the fast tempi are faster than when the great classical works were written. No one remains unaffected by the music he has heard or played.

The best way to study music is to hear a great deal of it. It makes no difference what sort of music you like. Great music is not neccessarily "serious" music. A waltz by Johann Strauss or a song by Gershwin are certainly great music. So is a Negro spiritual. The first collection of these spirituals, called *Slave Songs of the United States* was published in 1867. All over the world these spirituals are now accepted as part of the folklore of America. And a great deal of "serious" music has been written in the United States since. There was Charles Ives (1874–1954) who anticipated the atonalism of Schoenberg. When Georges Antheil's *Ballet mecanique* was performed in New York in 1927 (it was done by eight pianos, battery and several non-musical machines) there was naturally a scandal.

The United States has the advantage of accepting composers from Europe (Stravinsky, Ernest Bloch, Hindemith, Darius Milhaud,

Schoenberg) whose works are first performed here, and whose ideas often blend with those of native Americans who study in Europe for a while and come back with new impressions. This is what happened to Walter Piston, Aaron Copland, Roger Sessions, Roy Harris, Virgil Thomson, and others. No student of light opera can ignore such excellent works as Bernstein's *West Side Story* or *The Consul* by Gian-Carlo Menotti, who came from Italy to the United States.

No American composer has caught the soul of the country as well and beautifully in his music as George Gershwin. The time will soon come when *Porgy and Bess* will be called a sort of "American national opera." And Gershwin's *An American in Paris* and *Rhapsody in Blue* are enthusiastically received all over the world as the expression of a new, genuinely American music.

Gershwin's masterpiece Porgy and Bess *is frequently revived. Here is Hirschfeld's sketch of the cast from the New York City Center production of 1963.*

EPILOGUE

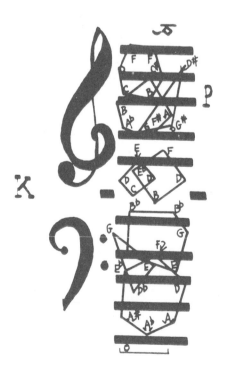

ART is always alive and changing, reflecting the constant change of life. In music, too, there is a constant flow of ideas, a continuous movement of undercurrents. The development of the long-playing record, of the tape recorder, of radio and television will have great impact on the development of music in the future. One of our great handicaps is that we don't know how the music really sounded until the beginning of our century. We have no proof exactly how Mozart and Beethoven wanted their symphonies played. But we do know how Richard Strauss, Benjamin Britten, or Igor Stravinsky wanted *their* music played; we have recordings made by these composers of their own music. Future generations will have authentic recordings of all music created since the 1920's.

Music belongs to everybody today. Gone are the days when only princes and cardinals, wealthy people and kings could afford the luxury of hearing a Haydn symphony or an opera by Monteverdi. There is music in almost every house in the Western world. Much of it is not serious music. But we know today that much serious jazz music is good music. We also know that much modern music, which is based solely on technical tricks, is not good music. Many composers are obsessed by uncertainty, they want to create something new for the sake of newness. I suppose you've heard "electronic" music—music made of sounds that are emitted by electric-frequency generators. To me this seems like trying to solve an artistic problem with the help of machines, as though it were a technical problem.

But who can tell? Some day computers may "compose" music. Perhaps this is the sound of the future.

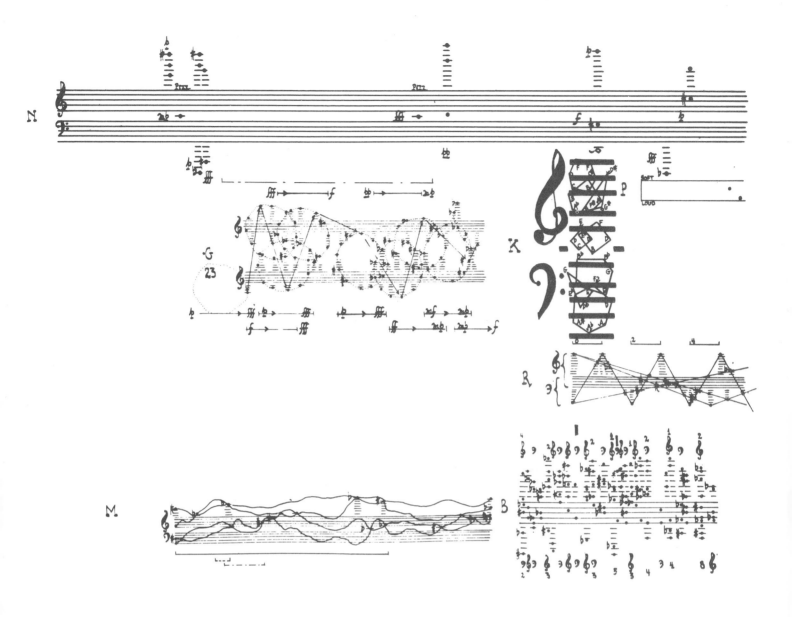

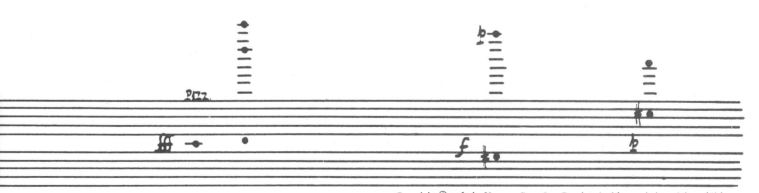

A page from Concert for Piano and Orchestra *by John Cage. Modern innovations in rhythm, tonality, form, and every other aspect of composition, have outgrown traditional notation. The examples on these pages illustrate the means by which contemporary composers have tried to express their musical ideas.*

GRATEFUL ACKNOWLEDGEMENT IS MADE FOR USE OF ILLUSTRATIONS:

Alinari-Art Reference Bureau: 10

Archiv für Kunst und Geschichte: 64

Herzog August Bibliothek, Wolfenbüttel: 29

Beethoven-Haus, Bonn: 92

The Bettmann Archive, Inc.: 18, 23 (left), 48, 53 (right), 62, 65, 68, 70, 71, 80, 87, 95 (top), 115 (top left), 116, 125 (right), 127, 130

Bildarchiv d. Ost. Nationalbibliothek: 78, 80, 82, 105 (bottom)

The British Museum: 43

The Brooklyn Museum: 63

The Cleveland Museum of Art: Copyright page (Leonard C. Hanna Bequest), 22 (left, Purchase from the J. H. Wade Fund), 31 (Gift from various donors by exchange)

Cliché Paul Bijtebier, Brussels: 35

Deutsche Musikgeschichtliche Archiv, Kassel: 49, 72, 74, 77

Fitzwilliam Museum, Cambridge: 15

Foto Ursula Seitz-Gray, Frankfurt: 21

Henmar Press Inc., New York: 138, 139

Kunsthalle Mannheim: 118

Kunsthistorisches Museum, Vienna: 75 (top)

The Metropolitan Museum of Art: 12 (Rogers Fund), 17 (bottom, Rogers Fund), 40 (Bequest of Annie Bolton Matthews Bryant), 54 (Harris Brisbane Dick Fund)

The Pierpont Morgan Library: 23 (right), 24, 57

Musée de Dijon: 65

Museo di S. Maria del Fiore, Florence: 16, 30

Museo Teatrale alla Scala, Milan: 115 (top left)

Museum Antiker Kleinkunst, Munich: 14

Collection of The Museum of Modern Art, New York: 129 (Lillie P. Bliss Collection), 136

National Museum, Rome: 13

The National Portrait Gallery, London: 61

The New York Public Library:

Music Division 48: (bottom), 50, 53, 54 (left), 73, 90, 93, 96, 98, 100 (top), 102, 105 (top), 107 (top), 117 (top left), 117 (bottom left), 119 (bottom), 120, 122, 124 (left), 128, 131 (bottom right), 134, 135

Picture Collection: 11 (bottom left), 17 (top), 19 (top), 19 (bottom), 20, 25 (top), 27, 28, 32, 33, 34, 37 (bottom), 38, 42, 46, 58, 59, 69, 85, 86, 88, 89, 94, 98, 99 (bottom), 100 (bottom), 101 (bottom left), 103 (left), 110 (left), 110 (right), 111 (left), 111 (right), 112, 117 (bottom right), 117 (top right), 119 (top), 126, 131 (top left), 137

Prints Division: Title Page, Prologue, 25 (bottom), 66, 84, 103

Photographie Giraudon, Paris: 11 (top), 37 (top), 44, 45, 78, 104, 123 (left)

Rijksmuseum, Leiden: 11

Schott's Söhne, Werbeabteilung: 131 (bottom left)

Arnold Skolnick: 26, 67, 79, 91, 109, 113

Staatliche Museen Zu Berlin: 99 (top)

Thur. Landes-Bibliothek, Weimar: 75 (bottom)

Tiroler Landesmuseum Ferdinandeum, Innsbruck: 47